SAY WHAT?

new words around town

KEITH BARKER-MAIN

metro

Published by Metro Publishing, an imprint of John Blake Publishing Ltd,
3 Bramber Court, 2 Bramber Road,
London W14 9PB, England

www.blake.co.uk

First published in hardback in 2006

ISBN-13: 978 1 84358 165 9
ISBN-10: 1 84358 165 5

British Library Cataloguing-in-Publication Data:

A catalogue record for this book is available from the British Library.

Design by www.envydesign.co.uk

Printed in Great Britain by Creative Print and Design

1 3 5 7 9 10 8 6 4 2

Papers used by John Blake Publishing are natural, recyclable
products made from wood grown in sustainable forests.
The manufacturing processes conform to the environmental
regulations of the country of origin.

Every attempt has been made to contact the relevant copyright-
holders, but some were unobtainable. We would be grateful if
the appropriate people could contact us.

This book is dedicated to the memory of my
ever-supportive mother, Augusta

ACKNOWLEDGEMENTS

Mindful of the TV car crash that was Halle Berry's excruciating 2002 Oscar acceptance speech, I'll try to keep this short.

I'd like to thank coolhunter extraordinaire and ex-*METRO LIFE* editor Elaine Paterson, who, inexplicably believing that I somehow have my finger on the social pulse, cajoled me into becoming a regular lifestyle columnist on Britain's brightest morning read. Thanks to overall 'heid bummer', Kenny Campbell, to Siobhan Murphy (who stepped into Elaine's size-six Miu Miu mules) and to all at *METRO* for their support. I would also like to thank the paper's acerbic resident foodie Marina O'Loughlin, a long-time pal and staunch ally. To Elizabeth Costa, my Hollywood agent (I just *had* to drop that in), ta, darl', for sorting out the publishing deal – on which note, cheers to Mark Hanks and to all at John Blake! I am very grateful to Penny Edwards, Alison Rae, Craig Pearson and Jon Ronson for their helpful advice.

I'd also like to thank my stylist, my hairdresser, my personal trainer, the universal life force and... cut to orchestra playing and gorillas in black suits hustling author off stage.

CONTENTS

INTRODUCTION

Day after day, I encountered them in a carefully choreographed ballet on the broad pavement outside my local Underground station. Nothing, it seemed, would deter them: rain, snow, freezing fog, potential attack by any of the neighbourhood's large and volatile nutter population, the health implications of hanging out on one of London's most traffic-clogged, polluted arteries... nothing! I began to think they would out-cockroach the cockroaches if Osama's turban-clad lieutenants wiped our wonderful city off the face of the Earth in some nuclear Armageddon.

For these were the days when Londoners seemed to pull together as one in the face of a new menace. In the months after 9/11, everyone seemed that little bit more compassionate towards their fellow man – a mood that had not gone unnoticed by the suits at major charity organisations. Their opportunistic marketing wheeze was to flood the streets with armies of clipboard-waving recruits in gaily coloured tabards, their smiley shiny young faces reminiscent of those persistent hookers for Scientology that used to reel in the unsuspecting passer-by with an offer of a free personality test at one of L Ron Hubbard's city-centre bureaux.

At first, I fell for their fundraising spiel. How could any bleeding heart not sign up to such worthy causes: the deaf; the blind; the homeless; medical research; starving children in Africa; stray dogs and people with deep-rooted depression on account of living in Hull, Barrow-in-Furness, Motherwell or Basingstoke, or being saddled from birth with names like Wayne, Shayne and Kylie-Storm. But, as the ink on my bank statements turned red, I feared I would either need to get another full-time job to support my philanthropic largesse, or risk becoming a charity case in my own right.

After conducting some research into these clipboard clowns I had assumed to be altruistic volunteers, it emerged their missionary zeal and Rottweiler-like reluctance to let go of anyone who fell in to their clutches was fuelled by the sort of commissions City stockbrokers would not turn their cocaine-raddled noses up at. My initial sympathy for these benevolent beggars turned to outright contempt and, talking to friends and colleagues, I realised I was not alone.

'It feels like we are being taken to the cleaners by a bunch of charity muggers... CHUGGERS, in fact,' I moaned to my then editor on daily newspaper *METRO*. And so the name for this grabby gang was coined.

We decided to bring this and other new buzzwords to the attention of *METRO* readers throughout the UK in a tongue-in-cheek column called 'SAY WHAT' (new words around town) that would be dedicated to identifying and naming emerging trends and cultural phenomena, particularly in the fields of fashion, marketing, the media and entertainment, and, although some of the inclusions in this anthology were already in use within those industries, the majority are the product of one overactive and undertaxed mind; ideas that would invariably go 'front of brain', most inconveniently, in the middle of the night.

Fast forward to the end of 2004. Eighteen months after 'chuggers' appeared in print in *METRO* and had been picked up on by columnists and commentators such as Alison Pearson in the *Evening Standard*, up pops etymologist Susie Dent on all the TV evening-news bulletins, declaring it to be one of the key new dictionary entries of the year ('origin unknown', I seem to remember her saying, much to my amusement).

So here's 'chuggers' along with over six hundred other must-use *bons mots* to add vim to your vocabulary. Become an early adopter and impress your friends with your on-the-zeitgeit-ness by peppering your conversation with some of the hottest new words around town.

Got a few of your own? Then let me know! I might just run them in the column... and there's always *Say What 2* to fill! E-mail me at: say.what.kbm@hotmail.com

Say What? Say these...

1

ON THE PULL

DATING AND MATING

Alarmed Call

The early-morning, hungover, panic call to your best friend, who might just have a handle on the events of last night and the name of the freak now hogging your duvet

Alcopuppies

She may dress twenty-five, but she's only just turned fifteen. Buy her another Bacardi Breezer at your peril. Her old man is a 6ft 3in chav bruiser. Still interested?

Alpha Editing

Tragically, still single, you vow to avoid being waylaid by unsuitable one-night stands (no matter how cute) on your route to Mr Alpha Male. Not exactly easy as ABC though, is it? Especially when you've already spent over a quarter of a century looking

Arm Bruiser

Walking out with a serious piece of rough in a tux. The ultimate accessory for a film premiere or A-list bash. Ray Winstone and Colin Farrell are way too sweet. Think really RUFF

Minx on the make looking for
a walking meal ticket.
'What's the attraction with that boring saddo?'
'Strictly ATM, he's a 24/7 Johnny Cash Dispenser.'

Bland Dating

Going out with vanilla-looking, insipid
(and minted) guys, because they make
you look fabulous and are always good for a
table at The Ivy

Bolly Dolly

She looks like Lambrini would be too good for her
but, when the drinks are on you, hers is always
expensive Champagne. Oops! You just pulled a
gold-digging Bolly Dolly

Boomerang Boyfriend

No matter how many times you chuck him,
he just keeps coming back. Duck and
you'll miss him (hopefully)

4

Bottle Blank

You've pulled. Back home, you open
the fridge only to be met by a Bottle Blank.
Your annoying flatmates have glugged the
emergency vino supply. 'Care for a Nescafé?'
you offer apologetically

Brekkie Reccie

4am. Your flatmate rolls in wasted and it
sounds like she's pulled.
You can't wait for the Brekkie Reccie
and the chance to give the little Pop Tart and
her stud-muffin a good grilling

Buffet

Lad-speak for a bit of a slapper.
A cheap synthetic spread that goes
a long, long way… and we're not
talking margarine.

Bungalow

As in: 'Had a date with Bill from IT. Bungalow!'
(It's all going on downstairs, with
nothing up top)

Cab-Hookey Make-Up

Emerging from the back seat of a taxi after a
heavy snog, you fail to notice the date's David
Sylvian-style maquillage has transferred on to
your dial. Big in Japan – just looks plain trashy
over here, dude

Call Waiting

He said he'd call but 'the coffee's all gone
and you're down to your last cigarette'
(to quote KD Lang). Watching the phone won't make
it ring, but we know the feeling

Carat Dangler

Nightclub diamond geezer whose promise of big rocks from Tiffany will turn to cut-price at Elizabeth Duke (if you're lucky) the minute he get his rocks off

Carbon Dating

What do those buff blonde twenty-something clotheshorses actually see in their prehistoric partners? Let's ask multimillionaire rock fossil Rod Stewart to let us in on his secret

Cereal Offender

You stumble down to breakfast only to find the flatmate's latest squeeze – a total pig that puts you off your cornflakes. Give that Cereal Offender a Frostie reception. It's enough to reduce your nerves to Shreddies

Cheese Plant

Sophisticated laddish pincer movement. Mate chats up bird in a cheesy manner that makes Alan Partridge seem sexy by comparison. Positioning yourself over his shoulder, you smile sympathetically at her and roll your eyes at his corny spiel. In no time at all, the victim will body swerve him and fire straight into you, convinced you're an altogether more sensitive soul

Claims Underwriter

A bezzie mate who unfailingly backs up your statement that you spent the night with them, when you were off being your usual dirty stop-out self

Costume Drama

Been through the entire wardrobe, but you still look like Queen Victoria or Quentin Crisp? Costume Drama! You'll never pull looking like that

Cross Dressing

'So last season! Makes me look fat! He's seen it before!' you wail angrily. You're late for a date and still in your pants, as the Cross Dressing reject pile becomes a mountain

Desperate Mousewives

Golf widowed in a gated complex with curtain-twitching piranhas as neighbours, you haunt internet chat rooms in search of romance. Is a mock-Georgian mansion and unlimited Prada a suitable trade-off for marital monotony? Time to escape the Desperate Mousewife trap

Dialemma

The new squeeze said he'd call, but hasn't yet. Ring him and appear desperate, or risk losing your potential Mr Right. You start to key in his number then chicken out, caught up in a Dialemma

Dose Candy

Not someone with a heavy cold talking about
Charlie. It's the type of loose-living female your
mother would deem 'not quite our sort, dear'.
You gave the performance of your life and she
just gave you the clap

Emotional NightCap

'I said all the wrong things. He's still not
over his ex. He's bound to chuck me, etc.'
Pouring some stiff Dutch courage, you call a
mate at midnight for some reassurance

Ex Directory

Bond Street stationers Smythson's
'Blondes Brunettes & Redheads' notebook
is the cad-around-town's bible, containing the
form on every filly he's ever squired. 'Need a
date for Ascot. Might have to go Ex Directory'

The Ex Factor

You just can't help comparing him to your ex. Bin those rose-tinteds! Meaner than Simon Cowell, a face like Louis Walsh's and shorter than Sharon Osbourne doesn't sound much like talent to us!

Ex-Messaging

Let's face it, hon, you've been dumped and no amount of silly texts will get them back. U R 2 2 :-(

Fatmate

Bridget Jones lookalike roomie you only hang around with in public because she makes you look like a supermodel by comparison

Flee-ancé

Whirlwind romance and the engagement ring is barely on her finger before you realise she's stacking up to be a retread of Kathy Bates's character in Misery. Leg it while you still can

Florist Grump

You feel so guilty when Interflora delivers a huge bouquet from your beloved, but you can't get past 'I loathe roses and yellow is so common'. Relax! We all get the Florist Grump

Foxymoron

Sure, she looks hot, but animal magnetism isn't everything. Trust us, she has the mind of a mange tout

not to be confused with

Poxymoron

Calls you daily then goes AWOL for a week. Acts sweet and sour. He won't introduce you to his mates and still hasn't given you his mobile number. What's to figure out? Just dump the Poxymoron!

Freight Train

A female that comes on way too strong. Given half a chance, she'll railroad her way into your life. Stay on track by shunting her straight into the sidings before your life hits the buffers

Friskicuffs

Phwoar! You're in for a bout of outrageous slap and tickle. It's Friskicuffs when she pulls out her marabou-trimmed manacles and clamps your wrists to the bedstead!

Henmania

Nowt to do with a certain Wimbledon underachiever. We're talking squawking birds out on the pull and dragged up like trick–or–treaters. Believe us, ladies, you're no treat and you won't be tricking us into buying you drinks all night

The Hickey Mickey

Oops! The love bite you thought you'd concealed so well is somehow glowing like a flashing neon sign. Now the whole office is taking the Hickey Mickey. Cover up that rash, trash! That's what polo necks were invented for

Honey Laundering

Your new bit of rough has no visible means of support and a three-stretch for fraud on the CV. Introducing him to the gang as 'something in the City', you indulge in a spot of Honey Laundering

Humpy Dumpy

A night of passion, numbers exchanged but still no call? Forget any fairytale ending, you've been given the Humpy Dumpy. Now put yourself together again!

Hyper-dating

Speed dating is so lame. Hyper-dating means having so many parallel paramours you're permanently shagged out

Jackie O No Moment

You're out on the razz and, after a few, you hit the powder room. You'd imagined yourself as a soignée young Jacqueline Kennedy, but the mirror reflects a spooky resemblance to Sly Stallone's scary Ma. It's a Jackie O No Moment!

Juicer

Beware of the new girlfriend steering you towards Selfridges' designer section. She's a high-maintenance Juicer and she'll squeeze the pips out of you. Fruity little minx!

Junk Bonding

Champagne Charlie City boys copping off with on-the-make scrubbers that congregate at every flash-trash gaff in town

Last Dance Chancer

Half the club has knocked him back and, at chucking-out time, he grabs you for a smooch to James Blunt's 'Beautiful'. By the time the lights go on, he's convinced you you're Gisele Bundchen and you want to have his babies. Still falling for the Last Dance Chancer shtick?

Lobal
Warming

Temperatures are rising and your latest
hottie is nuzzled up to your ear.
Who said Lobal Warming was all bad?

Lingergrei

Out for a few after work, you pull a George
Clooney clone and, on the point of passion, you
realise your slung-'em-on-in-a-hurry pants are
greyer than the Hollywood heartthrob's barnet.
Insist on doing it in the dark and make a mental
note to chuck out all your drab Lingergrei

Lounge Leper

Repulsive, reptilian nightclub lizards.
Dripping in jewellery, cologne
and cheap patter. To be avoided
like the plague

A Mantelpiece Job

Cute, decorative and ornamental
young man. A Mantelpiece Job
should be popped above your fireplace,
admired and occasionally dusted down. Think
Cillian Murphy or Jake Gyllenhaal

The Meet Market

Ladette-speak for a less than salubrious
nightspot where the beef on offer is less than
prime – yet you still go for last orders, just on
the off chance

Money For Old Grope

It takes a certain class of girl to go there, but it's
amazing what can be endured when your
paunchy, septuagenarian, wig-wearing beau
features high on the Sunday Times Rich List

Multi Asking

Desperate or brave? Six babes in the bar have
knocked you back already, yet still you persevere.
Who said women were better at Multi Asking?

The Nanny State

She wears pelmet skirts and blue eye shadow, karaokes to Britney, flirts outrageously with your boyfriends and gets rat-arsed at the silver surfers' disco. But you excuse anything of your born-again-teenager gran. 'Don't mind her. It's just the Nanny State.'

No-Frills Ferrari

Take it from us, in the style stakes, your No-Frills Ferrari isn't exactly top gear. A bashed-up K-reg runabout is a far classier chassis than any yeuch-yellow, souped-up, middle-age Italian boy toy. Think Jeremy Clarkson

Off Menu

Someone that is now in a stable(-ish) relationship and no longer up for grabs. As in: 'Emma isn't hanging out with us any more since she went Off Menu.'

On the Eriksson

A bit on the side. In honour of a certain football manager's off-pitch scoring record: the entire affair conducted via a separate dedicated mobile phone. As in: 'I've been playing away from home On the Eriksson.' Get it Sven you can

Pacamac

A condom carried in your purse,
in case he doesn't come prepared.
Beats getting splashed

Penile Dementia

When you haven't had it for so long,
you've forgotten how to use it

Piranharama

A man-eater-infested cop-off joint teeming with
shoals of predatory pairs fishing for Mr Big.
Serves them right if all they catch is crabs

Pot F***

Not fussy. As long as you get off, you'll take a chance on anything. Life is a lottery after all

Present Tense

Those difficult moments as you start to unwrap your new squeeze's gift, dreading what you'll uncover might constitute a chuckable offence

Romantic Friction

A love life that is less Mills and Boon, more Gloom and Doom – guaranteed to rub you up the wrong way

Shag A Dog Story

Caned it and ended up with a bit of a canine?
Pure bow wow… serves you right for going
out dogging. Still, your mates will have a
good laugh about it at the pub, you manky
mutt magnet

Sheik 'N' Vac

Grubby Middle Eastern playboy
and his vacuous Versace-clad blonde arm
candy. She's with him for his looks, wit and
dazzling intellect, obviously

So! Sushi

Any nightspot that is a bit of a pickup joint.
The same tired old dishes go round
and round, conveyor-belt style, just
begging to be chosen. Not to be
confused with the similar-sounding
Japanese-style restaurant chain

Spewrious Behaviour

Sobering up as your wine bar Romeo moves in for the kill, you realise he's more Wayne Rooney than George Clooney. Spewrious Behaviour involves faking an upchuck in the loo and demanding he calls a cab to take you home (at his expense, obviously!). 'No really. I'll be fine. And I'd rather be alone, thanks.'

Stealth-Bombed

It starts with a toothbrush, make-up bag and tights, until, pretty soon, she's annexed your bachelor pad. You've been Stealth-Bombed, mate!

Stoned Cladding

Gold glitter wellies, white tutu, polka-dot tights and that puce poncho you dragged back from Mexico: oh dear, it really wasn't too clever to roll a reefer before you got dressed for the evening, was it?

Supermarket Sweep

Late-night cruising in the aisles of
Morrisons, Asda, Tesco and Sainsburys.
You'll be amazed at what's on special offer.
The tastiest takeaways shop at Waitrose,
however, don't even contemplate a Rod Lidl

Tongue 'n' Groove

The DJ's spinning smoochy R'n'B. Don't be a plank!
Nail that babe against the wall and get into some
serious Tongue 'n' Groove action

Uncle Slam

Wham, bam and not even so much as a
'thank you, ma'am'. Inconsiderate American
lover in a hurry. No stars and needs a stripe
tearing off

Upping the Auntie

Boffing your best mate's mother's foxy sister.
Here's to you, Mrs Robinson!

Wash and Go

A one-night stand that's in a hurry to
leave the next morning. Forget breakfast,
he just wants to Wash And Go

Whether Girl

'Which shoes do you like best?'
'Should I have my hair up or down?'
'What dress looks better?' Aaagh!
Don't get involved with a Whether Girl.
She'll rain on your day, sunshine

Yahooer

Trawling internet sites for a bit of
how's your father? Yahooer!

2

ON THE TOWN

FOR YOUR ENTERTAINMENT

Bad Movie

With the cinema now packed solid, your ill-considered decision to sit behind a high-haired, popcorn-munching, text-crazy, incessant chatterer was a bit of a Bad Movie

Bliggin

Dressing up large and crashing a major A-list do. The secret is never to stop at the red velvet rope. PR intimidation works!

Bloc-listed

Super-expensive (tacky) nightclubs colonised by the Russian Mafia and icy blonde hookers from former Eastern Bloc countries. U.So.So.R. not going!

Borderline Smoker

Scots who regularly pop over to a pub beyond Hadrian's Wall just to be able to light up without shivering outside in the driving rain. Not for long... England gets stubbed out in 2007

Cabracadabra

Cold, wet and miles from home on deserted late-night streets? Just say 'Cabracadabra' and a yellow light on a black roof magically appears. Works every time

Carte Fixed

Have the restaurant fax over the menu and order in advance, leaving you free to sparkle wittily at the dinner table while others wade through the options

Clipboard Angel

You're wasted after all night clubbing and miles from home in a taxi-free zone when, out of nowhere, a vision in a black puffa coat magically appears and adds your name to her minicab list. Clipboard Angel sent from Heaven

Chippy Clippie

Intimidating 'greeter' at hot bar/restaurant. Black-clad clipboard Nazi with all the charm and finesse of Goebbels. Lighten up! You're just a glorified receptionist dear

Compulsive Flyers

OK! So you lied and you've never actually been to a Ragga Revival Roadblock, but who can resist those funky mini artworks littering every bar in town?

Dagenham Dodgem

You know you shouldn't. But come club chucking-out time, with nary a taxi in sight, the minicab tout is a tempting shout, as you risk a Dagenham Dodgem ride home

Door Stopper

Black-clad gorilla that prevents you from crashing the VIP area. Forget it, who wants to hang out with a bunch of X Factor rejects anyway?

Footie Tootie

Why is every swanky club loo cubicle permanently engaged? Because half the Premiership and their floozies have scored some Footie Tootie. Red card 'em!

Gratuities Violence

A tenner for a cocktail and service included as extra, yet still those Mojito muggers leave the gratuities line open. We say deduct the 12.5% as a matter of principle

Hari Karaoke

What you feel like committing when some bawling banshee gets up to murder Robbie's 'Angels' for the tenth time in one evening

Intercourse

The polite term for the new ritual of nipping
off with someone you scarcely know for…
a quick fag on the pavement between
main course and pudding at
some health fascist's smoke-free
restaurant

Homepride Man
Your friendly(-ish) black-clad club
doorman whose real role is to sift
the wheat from the chav

Loo Locust
Someone who scoops up chewing gum,
lollipops, matches, perfume, condoms and
every other goody that is laid on in ritzy
nightspot bathrooms, just because they're free

Plastic Surgery
In need of a good night out? Grab the old man's
Amex, give yourself a lift and indulge in some
painless Plastic Surgery

Queudos

Sashay straight past waiting wannabes, dazzle the door whore with your urban fabulousness and watch that velvet rope open. You so know you got Queudos, baby!

Smoke Alarm

The growing sense of panic experienced by Woodbine addicts as they wonder how the hell they'll manage a social life when bars, clubs and restaurants and now even the ruddy pavement, it seems, go ciggie-free in 2007

Snorah Jones

Wine bar owners and dinner-party hosts take note. Chill-out CDs are sleep-inducing bores! Think (s)Norah Jones. And, no, we do not want to hear (dead-as-a-) Dido either!

Stool Pigeons

Bartender speak for plump cocktail-chugging birds roosting on hard-to-find stools at the latest hotspot in town

Whine Bar

You fancy a Pouilly Fumé, but find yourself surrounded by thirty-somethings necking Chardonnay while moaning about their relationships (or lack of...). More Whine Bar than wine bar

3

ON THE HOUSE

PROPERTY DEVELOPMENTS

A Little
Bit Linda

Style-guru putdown. As in: 'Darling, aren't
those repro Deco cream leather sofas and
matching pouffes just a little bit Linda?'
Bland blonde Barker!

Ag and Kim

New Cockney slang for grim, as in manky/minging.
'Looked at a bedsit in West Ham. Bit Ag and Kim.'
How clean is your house?

Agamama

So she finally got her dream country cottage?
Too clueless to cope with the Aga,
in desperation, the urban mama bungs
a supermarket meal in the microwave
and claims she's been slaving over a
hot stove all day

Amuse Bush

Upmarket gardening trend for 'hilarious'
topiary. You think a foliage dog cocking
a leg against a wall is funny?
Leaf it out!

similarly

Amuse Bouche

Lower-facial topiary of the type favoured by
George Michael. Goatee beards make
you look like, er, a goat. But we're très
amused by your bouche, mush

Bad Catmosphere

You may be oblivious to the odour of Tiddles's litter tray and feline fishy lunch-bowl contents. But, take it from us, your flat will not sell so long as there's a Bad Catmosphere

similarly

Catastrophy

Arriving at a posh do wearing a Little Black Dress covered in kitty moult is a sartorial Catastrophy. Give the brush off to our number one pet hate

Beij-ing

Not this year's upmarket interior fad for chinoiserie, more the TV-makeover mandarins' Communist-like push to paint everything in ten shades of bland. We are so beyond beige, darling!

Bingo Brainer

Numbers obsessive with property-price Tourette's syndrome, ranting about the ups and downs of the market. Not quite a full house!

Chippy

Student-speak for very cheap digs. Inspired by Tango-tone TV antique David Dickinson's catchphrase 'Cheap as chips'. As in: 'I'm sharing a flat out in the sticks. Bit of a grot squat, but nice 'n' chippy.'

D.I.Why?

'Faaab-u-lus' tricks with MDF, stencils and collages? Moroccan boudoir or Suzie Wong opium den themes? Vile! Gruesome twosome, er, interior designers Justin Ryan and Colin McAllister are the kings (queens?) of this silly makeover mayhem

Decorneckers

The bane of estate agents' lives, downmarket Ideal Homer property tourists, who fancy a free Sunday nose at high-spec lifestyles

DFL

The reviled 'Down From London' brigade. Pricing resentful locals off their own turf, they snap up coastal cottages in Cromer, Camber Sands, Whitstable, Hastings and Southwold, inviting their braying townie mates down for the weekend and generally behaving as if they are still in Fulham

Dordogne Daydreamer

Yes, that off-the-beaten track hamlet you stayed in this summer was idyllic. But sell up and move there? Have you ever been to France in February? It makes a wet weekend in Walsall seem blissful by comparison

Eileen Graydar

The invisible antennae capable of sniffing out a genuine piece of priceless iconic designer furniture amid all that market-stall tat

Flatpack

A sniffy putdown to describe someone's home interior as a tad too IKEA self-assembly. As in: 'They may own a luxury penthouse, but their taste is pure Flatpack.'

Flock Mentality

We're so over those ubiquitous feature walls covered in sub-Tandoori flocked paper. Stop sheepishly following everything you see in makeover magazines!

Halston

Postcode snobs' designer 'village' names don't fool us. It's either Hackney or Dalston, whatever you call it

HEC

Hey trailer trash! A super-sized silver Home Entertainment Centre in your 'lounge' is beyond common and deeply naff. Pure HEC!

Herberts

Their state-of-the-art show-home kitchens are littered with pots of burnet, borage, comfrey and chervil plus rack upon rack of dried exotica even Gordon Ramsey would be hard pushed to identify. Yet the only seasoning the silly Herberts ever use are malt vinegar and Saxa

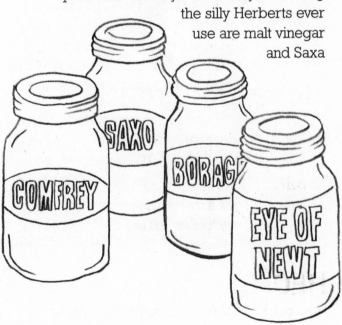

HiPod

The ultimate bachelor pad. A penthouse with terrace and city views: packed with plasmas, surround sound and flash gizmos you didn't even know had been invented – sadly not available on your £40-a-week rent budget, mate

Home Oh! Erotica

You enter the developers' carefully staged 'loft-style' apartment and gasp: Krug- stocked Smeg, Eames recliners, plasma screen, home gym, wet room and Harvey Nics bags everywhere. But it's still just a bland box on a brownfield site at the edge of town. Interior porn is such a turn-on though

'Hoodhype

Estate agents attempt to talk up unfashionable areas. As in: Harlesden/Moss Side/Possil Park/Knowsley? I don't think so, darling. It's all 'Hoodhype

Ikeahorrea

The unavoidable result of a total lack of control when faced with those irresistible bargains that lurk in the bowels of our favourite Swedish retailer is a house full of unwanted crap

Interior Resigned

Why fret over TV home-improvement design dictators' diktats? Your shabby-chic pad looks fine to us. Interior Resigned = stress-free living

Interiority Complex

Ashamed of your shabby-chic decor?
Watching DIY-design shows can lead to a
bad case of Interiority Complex. But what sane
person would let those odious home makeover
show 'gurus' loose on their pad?

Kitschens

Who wants granite work surfaces, sleek
stainless-steel appliances and acres of dark
wood? Strings of plastic fruit, raffia Chianti
bottle lamps, camp 50s diner furniture and
seaside holiday tiles are what's cooking in
smart homes now

Laminate Whores

DIY junkies who can't resist covering every available
floor-space in mock beech veneer. Glueless!

Lattefied

Formerly rundown hellhole neighbourhood that is on the up, as witnessed by an invasion of coffee chains such as Starbucks/Costa et al. As in: 'Prices have shot up since the old red-light district was Lattefied.'

The Loan Arranger

House prices on the up again? Time to call the mortgage broker and pronto, Tonto! Even a wigwam in Wigan is nudging 400K

Neighbores

Six-figure-salary job (yawn), Eton pleading for their brat to attend (sure!), holiday villa in hell being photographed for Homes & Gardens (like we care!)… time to feign a mystery infectious disease and bin those bragging 'bores

Ouch
Couch

Bumpy-lumpy-frumpy and downright uncomfy, that Ouch Couch has got to go. Chuck out the chintz, indeed

Panic Buying

Sell up and flee London because of potential terror wallahs? Please! To misquote Virginia Woolf, 'If it's a choice between Wiltshire and death, I choose death.'

Property
Barren

Still can't get your foot on the housing ladder? Welcome to the world of the Property Barren. But watch your friends' smugness turn to tears when the market turns and they need to offload that rapidly depreciating 'loft-style' pad in its 'lively inner-city setting'

Property Not-Spot

Don't believe the hype! That mock-Georgian gated complex overlooking the motorway and sink estate from hell will never be the new Chelsea. It's a Property Not-Spot

Property Porn

Townies' favourite country pastime: hitting some rural backwater estate agents and orgasming over sheaths of sexy sale particulars. 'Only £175k... What? For an entire house? We'll take it!'

Ryanheirs

A whole new generation of property owners set to inherit their folks' mini-chateaux five minutes away from some obscure French airstrip. But will the Ryanheirs be so smug if the routes get axed?

Ryjüt

Like one of our favourite Swedish flatpack-furnishing supplier's impossibly named, self-assembly units, Ryjüt is exactly what we feel like doing when we round the last corner and discover check-out queues longer than Bank Holiday weekend check-in desks at Gatwick

The Salivation Army

The bane of estate agents', car dealers' and designer shop assistants' lives. The Salivation Army wastes their time by slobbering over Portobello pads, Porsches and Prada, when their budgets barely stretch to Nissan, Newham and New Look

Sarf'ari

Your friends are getting 'so much space for the money' in some 'edgy' Sarf London urban jungle. King's Road is the furthest south you've ever been. With A to Z in hand, you point the Range Rover in the general direction and set off on Sarf'ari

Satellite City

Postcode snobs will only consider addresses where conservation-area status bans TV dish antennae. 'Stratford, Leith? Sparkbrook? Rusholme? Birkenhead? Never! Satellite City, darling.'

SHIC

Shoreditch, Hoxton, Islington, Clerkenwell… Notting Hill is just so last century. West ain't best

Six Packer

Greedy estate agents perk up in the presence of the Six Packer. A budget of one and six zeros or more? Welcome to Six Packer heaven, London's SW7 or Edinburgh's New Town most likely

Shamdelier

The real thing has become a design cliché, but, if you must, buy fake! You won't feel so guilty when it comes to chucking out a £60 plastic Shamdelier

Skipping

Late-night booty trawl
through builders' skips.
Memphis mirror,
Eames recliner. You'll be
amazed what people chuck out

Tadpole Flat

Greedy developer's conversion,
where a large, splashy reception
room tails off into woefully
puny cupboards posing
as bedrooms

Vanupmanship

The neighbours use Ocado.
Upping the stakes, you call Harrods
for home delivery. Talk about Vanupmanship!
Of course, a Lidl lorry outside would
be the ultimate reverse snobbery

Village Idiots

Gullible snobs that gladly pay over the odds
to live in an inner-city slum now rebranded
a village by greedy estate agents.
N.B. Abbeville is still Clapham South,
Brackenbury is only Hammersmith
and Mapesbury is plain
old Kilburn

4

ON HIGH STREET
NEAR YOU

NEW URBAN TRIBES

1661

Nothing to do with Kronenbourg lager. Skinny
Minnie dressing way too young: she looks 16
from behind and 61 from the front

Adulescent

Micro-scooters, skateboards, baseball caps,
PlayStations, 'kewl dude'-speak, CDs, etc.
Thirty-somethings as outsize children. Grow up!

Aspic Chick

Blue eye shadow, blonde Farah Fawcett hair,
micro mini, Abba accessories and the wrong
side of fifty? She's set in time-warp jelly,
a total Aspic Chick

Barbiecutie

So you think you're hot with your fresh-from-the-
sunbed-parlour glow? Take it from us, doll, that
barbecued tiger-prawn tan looks plain fishy

Basque Terrorist

The burlesque revival is fine, but
overpadded girlies exploding out of
too-tight corsets is so not da bomb

Beyoncé Beyond

Bootylicious bling bling honey. As in:
'Shizzle ma nizzle sista, you got it going on…
like totally Beyoncé Beyond'

Blitz Kidderz

The dire 80s rehash trash trend is fooling
nobody. Fancy yourself as some edgy fashion
icon from Steve Strange's legendary New
Romantic club? Sorry, but that Limahl crossed
with Bonnie Tyler pose just isn't working

BOBFOC

Body Off Baywatch, Face Off Crimewatch.
You know who you are!

Brandroid

A consumer whose existence revolves exclusively around multinational clone chains. There's life beyond the mall, doll

Burbie Doll

Buffed, immaculate, overdressed, suburban bimbo that finds Footballers' Wives aspirational. Middlesex, the Wirral, the West Midlands and Renfrewshire are chokka with these plastic Pats

Bürotrash

Obnoxious, loud office drones with ill-fitting suits, naff shoes and bad hair, swilling jugs of half-price Long Island Iced Tea with Aftershock chasers. All Bar One? Bar 'em all!

Caulie
Heads

White-haired grannies sporting
special-discount, too-tight perms.
'Stop at a Motorway Services? No way!
Can't get served for Caulie Heads.'

Chuggers

Licensed charity muggers with coloured
tabards and clipboards lying in wait on every
high street in the land to pounce on you and
relieve you of your dosh by pressing all
your guilt buttons and making you
sign up to their cause

Collagentry

Pampered rich women of a certain age who
just can't resist that rejuvenating Harley Street
instant facelift miracle prick. Spot them by their
telltale pincushion-faces

DAFTY

Divorcée Acting Far Too Young. Desperate middle-aged mothers out on the pull, dressed like their daughters. St Tropez, Marbella and Miami Beach are full of them, as is your local nightclub no doubt

Eton Mess

Drunken public-school brat acting lairy and obnoxious in upmarket nightclubs. Makes Harry Windsor and James Hewitt look like St Francis of Assisi by comparison

Florida Oranges

That radioactive sunbed glow is less St Tropez tan, more a case of Florida Orange. Looking like you've been Tangoed is beyond the pale, you daft old fruits

FoBo

Faux Bohemian. Just because you drink soy latte, read pretentious pseudo-intellectual novels and once went to Goa does not make you cred, you Westbourne Grove organic wasabi wazza

Gangsta Crappers

Shit Tupac wannabes. A pad in North Kensington, Sean John parka and sub-Ali G jive does not qualify you as ghetto fabulous, Rupert. Diss dat!

Gelly Baby

Bloke who slaps on so much hair product he ends up with that silly, shiny, plastic wig look going on. Just wash and go, you big Gelly Baby

Glazed And Confused

Mykonos, Malibu and Monte Carlo are chokka with international eye candy. Sure, they look like they walked out of a style-bible photo-shoot, but you'd get more sense out of your pet poodle than these fashion victim vacuums. Hoovery very sad

Greenpiss Artist

You lecture us on saving the whale, the ozone layer, sustainable resourcing and boycotting Tesco, then jump in your gas-guzzling SUV and drive fifteen miles and back to your nearest farmers' market. You taking the Greenpiss?

Harvey Nickalls

Chic boutique speak for those
artful dodgers who insist on not paying
for their designer gear. But would you
want to mess with those earpiece-totin'
bruisers in black on the door?

Hip Hoppers

Run DMC to the airport for a bargain
short-haul weekend to Europe's style capitals.
Bilbao, Dubrovnik, Krakow and Timosoara are
the current Hip Hoppers' fave raves

Hoodilum

Happy slappy thugs in crappy cappies. We're with
Bluewater shopping centre in Kent on this one.
Ban 'em! Hoodie you think you are, punk?

Jag Hag

Superannuated, St Tropez-tan-toting
dolly bird in her flash motor.
Luxury leather seats and matching skin

Joe Brand

Rag-trade-speak referring to a young
casual who will pay over the odds for any
piece of old tat, as long as it's plastered
with a billboard-sized logo. Fleece 'em!

Kappa Slappa

The Italian tracksuit is Vicky Pollard's leisure
apparel of choice. Need one say more?

Kid On
Cockney

West London public-school boy trying
to act street. Hugo, you went to Eton
not East Ham Comp, innit?

Lewisham Lifts

That common scraped-up ponytail and
hoop earring thang. Instant facelift?
Face like a ripped-out fireplace, more like

Label Louts

Porky, pasty footie hooligans decked
out in seriously expensive designer gear.
'Got a bit of a wardrobe crisis, mate.
Should I wear the pink Pucci or the
yellow YSL for that ruck with the Arsenal?'

Lippy Leslie

If you're contemplating bee-stung collagen lips, stop for a mo' and consider what happened to poor Leslie Ash. Ah! Thought not! Stick to luscious Lancôme lippy instead

LTC

Boutique speak for Last Chance Trendy. Should see-through kaftans, crop tops, bumster jeans and underwear as outerwear ever be contemplated by the over-40s? Discuss!

MallTeasers

Nubile, precocious teenage girls dressed like mini Moldovan hookers and hanging out in packs at the local indoor shopping centre. You can look, boys, but don't touch!

Mechanically Recovered Chicken

We don't care how much you spent at the salon, or how good your pins and boobs are: pushing fifty-five, Pamela Anderson blonde, in Jodie Marsh micro-mini and Liz McDonald-style décolleté makes you look like mechanically recovered chicken

Mosher

(From mosh-pit) Young neo-Goths
in a uniform of jumbo flared jeans and black
hooded sweatshirts emblazoned with Slipknot,
Limp Bizkit, Korn, Linkin Park and Marilyn
Manson logos. Tend to travel in packs

Nappsters

Vertical-arse lads in bumster jeans with crotches
worn nappy style and halfway down their legs.
It's not cute, you look like you've cacked
yourself, baby

Nobheads

Blokes in cream knitted beanies, worn low over the forehead. Looking like button mushrooms about to undergo surgery or, when teamed with a goatee, like Charles I on his execution day. Off with their heads!

Noseferatu

Spindly, creepy, coke-snorting vampire.
Think Docklands dinner party

Porsche Spice

Top rolled down and state-of-the-art sound
systems blaring, Daddy's little Mrs Beckham
wannabe princesses jam the roads in Essex,
Surrey, Cheshire and Dumbartonshire in
£100K's worth of gleam dream machine.
Jealous? Us? Makes us sicky Vicky

Puff Mummy

A swollen-faced woman of a certain age who just
can't say 'no' to collagen and Botox

Quorn
Flakes

Veggie, vegan, macrobiotic, tofutarian.
Whatever! We've had it with faddy food
fashions. Bring on hulking slabs of dead
cow and leave the daft diets to those crazy
Quorn Flakes

Raggamuppet

So you think you're da bomb with your souped-
up wheels, blacked-out windows and Pirate FM
booming at 150 DB? No, bro', you're just a
rankin' Raggamuppet

Rara Tara

Horrible 1980s fashtrash revival: appliqué, shoulder
pads, leg warmers and tiered mini skirts. Sorry,
Blondie, you're just a Rara Tara

Reverse Oreo

Named after the popular American cookie.
Someone who's white on the outside but is
more ghetto fabulous at heart than 50 Cent,
André 3000, Missys E and Dynamite-he-he
put together

Robbin' Hoodies

What made Marian anxious?
Those robbin' hoodies loitering around the
shopping precinct waiting to mug
old ladies, that's what

Saga Louts

Over sixty, overseas and over the top.
Pissed-up pensioners at Pontins. Grannies
from Grimsby on the grab in Gran Canaria.
Dodgy codgers out for a roger in Rimini.
Maybe we'll try Eastbourne this year for
a bit of peace

Seam Queen

Has she or hasn't she had a lift?
That telltale tuck behind the ears will
let you know if she has joined the
Seam Queens

Sloane Squares

Named after Chelsea's central piazza,
these braying minor public-school dimwit
fogey fossils are the reason why you should
avoid the Caribbean in winter and The
Cotswolds at all times

Sloburbans

What's with the outer postcodes' slobby leggings,
T-shirt and tacky trackies fixation?
Sartorial sloppiness sends us into a
Slough of despondency

Snoutcasts

The Nanny State-imposed smoking
ban sets up a new social category:
Marlboro Men and Gauloises Girls
forced to light up al fresco are
Snoutcasts – what a drag

Sticker Stacker

A supermarket trolley piled high with orange
'reduced price' items is the telltale sign of a
Sticker Stacker – a savvy shopper with an eye
for a deep-freezeable discount deal

Stinky Minkys

Like the old slogan said, 'It takes
several dumb animals to make this
coat but just one to wear it.' It's back
but fur still stinks, you sad minx. Got it?

Stretch Princesses

Tanked-up screeching secretaries on a city-centre bar crawl in a long white car. Hired limos are so trailer trash

Sugar Plum Scarys

Dressing up all cute pink, fluffy and sparkly to match your eight-year-old daughter is just plain frightening, you Sugar Plum Scary

Tofu Toffs

Minted Glastonbury-going macrobiotic, eco-conscious Trustafarians who hug trees and sponsor whales, yet drive gas-guzzling coupes, wear child-labour-sweatshop designer duds and pay the maid 75p an hour. Tossy Tofu Toffs

Trainer Trash

Vicky Pollard prototype. You'll recognise
them by the foghorn voice, tight
scraped-up hair, hoop earrings, track
pants and those ubiquitous white swoosh
trainers. Usually answers to the name
of Chelseigh, Cortnee, Holleigh or Ashleigh

Trophy Sophie

Mercenary minx on the make. She insists on a
boyfriend who will keep her in bling:
Balenciaga, Boucheron, Bolly, Barbados and
Bentleys. Expensive habit but is she worth it?

The Warsaw Pack

Ever-closer European integration?
We say 'tak!' to cute and capable plumbers,
builders, sparks and gardeners from East
of The Elbe. Poles apart from the
cowboy competition

The Wizened Of Oz

Fair skin and too many rays are never a good
combo. Take a leaf out of Nicole Kidman's book
and slather on the Factor 40, or end up like
crocodile (Dundee) skinned Paul Hogan

Yankers

On a one-to-one basis, we love them, mostly,
but how come whenever Americans travel en
masse they turn into loud, brash, bragging,
whiny Yankers?

5

ONLINE

AND OTHER TECHIE STUFF

Bashing the Hash

Impotent rage as you punch the touch-tones in
call-centre-hold hell. An old-fashioned dial
phone, sans hash key, guarantees a human
response in seconds.

Try it!

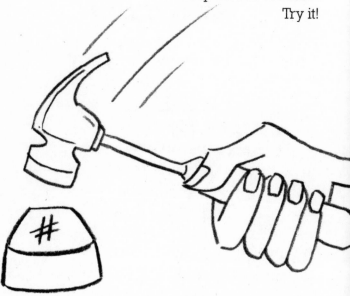

Anorakxia

Stultifying factoids about the SFX
in the next Spielberg flick; Clarkson-esque
aperçus on the latest Lamborghini; 4-4-2
versus 3-4-3 formations; the merits of
Apple's new operating system; unpicking
The Da Vinci Code: he's suffering from a sad
case of Anorakxia

Blackberry Crumble

You thought you had it all in the palm of
your hand, but when your groovy gadget
went AWOL your universe crumbled.
Should have backed up your life
elsewhere, you silly pudding

Crackberries

Oh yes! Blackberrys are amazing
but they can prove highly addictive

Cyberchondria

Fear of the internet. Honest, you
daft Luddite, it's E Z PC!

Expensive Mistech

Palm pilot, camcorder and all-singing-and-
dancing phone. Seemed like a good idea at the
time, but six months on it languishes untouched
in its box – Expensive Mistech

Fadgets

Must-have techie toys that fall out of fashion:
8-Track cartridges; Sega Dreamcast; DAT recorders;
Betamax... how long before MP3 players end up
as museum pieces?

Fear of Attachment

Scared to click on that
Inbox paperclip sign?
The big bad virus might
gobble your hard drive?
You're suffering Fear of
Attachment

Google Eyed

The blurry interlude before
your peepers refocus after
hours spent searching
on the net

Igno-rant

Cretinous one-sided, loud mobile monologue. Utterly tedious to listen in on and plain rude. Yes, we know you're 'on the train', you muppet!

iPod Shuffle

Moseying along to the beat of the music then stopping suddenly to change playlists so we walk slap bang into you

Laptop Dancer

She's constantly making out with her gorgeous new iBook, so you'll need some sexy new moves to win back the attention of your Laptop Dancer. Of course, you could just hit the pub. Like she'd notice!

Macintosher

Sad nerd who drones on interminably
about the merits of the Apple of his eye.
PC off, geek boi! You're giving us the pip!

Minimailism

**A relationship reduced to communicating
entirely via one-liners... C U@ 8 @ Urs M8.
Outlook Express or what?**

Mobile Macarena

A phone rings and suddenly everybody's
involved in a choreographed routine
checking to see if it's theirs

Mousefrau

Why schlep around Tesco with the whining
rugrats when you can order it all online?
Tea and scones and Price Drop TV – Ah!
The joy of being a Mousefrau

MTS

Mobile Tourette's Syndrome. Yelling into
your hands-free as you lurch
down the high street looks ever
so slightly bonkers, dear

Nerdvana

Tell your geeky boyf that spending Saturday
afternoon prowling four floors of retail space
devoted entirely to computer games and
software is not your idea of bliss

Netiquette

The dos and don'ts of online chatting.
CAPITALS ARE THE EQUIVALENT OF SHOUTING

nITwit

Are we simply clueless nITwits or do all IT product manuals assume the reader has a degree in advanced gobbledygook?

Nomo

Power people are ditching their mobiles and Blackberries, as 24/7 accessibility is so common. Nomos say 'Ring my PA!'

Percussive Maintenance

Repeatedly banging the keyboard, or whacking
the TV until they function again is the low-tech
solution for temperamental equipment

Predictive Texlexia

You meant to say 'Wanna go shopping?' but the
text gets sent as 'Wanna go shagging?'
Footballers' wives get it wrong every time

Sexy Texy

Joyless journey, mind-numbing meeting or
turgid tutorial? An outrageously flirty SMS
message to the squeeze will liven it up.
Sexy Texys push all the right buttons

Technotwat

Obsessing about operating systems, Skype,
firewalls, WAP phones and pixels is for sad
anoraks. Airport? What?
Stanstead or Luton?

Text Tart

Moronic mobile addict.
Their entire life revolves around
bombarding people with sad, pointless
and unfunny text messages

Textual Obsessive

During dinner, at the cinema, on
the beach, when they are taking a call
on their landline and probably when
they're in the sack, the Textual Obsessive
is at it like an SMS bunny

Tone Def

Eminem (lardy sales rep); Gnarls Barkley
(estate agent); Kylie (cheesy air steward);
Pussycat Dolls (bimbo sunbed operator);
Crazy Frog (the clinically brain dead): those
loony tunes mobiles are
driving us nuts, you ring-
Tone Def renegade

Vendetta

Bearing a grudge against or physically attacking an inanimate object that took your £1 and failed to dispense a Coke is irrational. It's just a vending machine, for Pete's sake

Vidididdy

You set the video to record the Arsenal v Man U game, but somehow you've ended up with Songs Of Praise and The Antiques Roadshow. Get the manual out, you Vidididdy

Virtual Recluse

Look fit, still have all your own teeth but spending all your time on computer games or in chat rooms? Get a real life, you mousebound stop-in

6

ON THE BOX

IN THE MAGS, AT THE MOVIES

The (Anthea) Turner Prize

Awarded to the most overexposed TV presenter, who should now be banished to cable-channel obscurity. And the nominees are: Sharon Osbourne, Natasha Kaplinsky, Simon Cowell, Jimmy Carr and Cat Deeley

Beckstabbers

Knives are well and truly out for Britain's best-loved brand. Once sycophantic journos are putting the boot in to the ex-captain and his matchstick missus. They smile in your face, all the time they wanna take your place, the Beckstabbers

Bling Bland Blonde

Rocks and frocks photo-op junkies.
Interchangeable tabloid fodder.
Surely not Alicia Douvall, Isabella Hervey,
Victoria Silvstedt, Paris H or the Olsen twins?

Buckraking

Digging for dirt on a D-list celeb from a friend whose second cousin does their hair, so you can flog it for a few bob to a tabloid gossip column

Celebrititty

(Double) G-lister
whose fame stems
from flashing her
baps at the
paps. Jodie, Jo
and Jordan,
Mammary mia!

Channibalism

Brain-dead TV execs
regurgitating other
station's shows:
How long before
What Not To Wear For A Wife Swap?
Paul Danan Test Drives Your Nanny?
Celebrity Car Boot Sale On Ice?
How Clean Is Your Camp Decorator?

Chefebrity

We are so over TV cooks as superstars.
Only Delia qualifies. Gordon, Nigella,
Gary Ainsley and AWT, sling your
(butcher's) hook, luvvy!

Cruise Control

Maintaining a rigid grip on your PR image, à la
Tom Cruise. So how come his people didn't
manage to block South Park's 'Tom Cruise Is In
The Closet' sketch – a scurrilous and wholly
unjustified lampooning of this red-blooded
regular male and a fine father to boot – from
becoming a cult Net mpeg giggle?

Dicklit

Male equivalent of chicklit. The sort of read that
makes Nick Hornby seem like Flaubert. Pulp fiction
for the lads (also Pricklit – much the same but with a
hand-shandy special on every second page)

Eamonn Holmeboys

Podgy, dodgy, Irish boy bands. You know who you are... so do us a favour and beat it back to Blarneyland with those Dublin Chins!

Em 'n' em

The ubiquitous Tracey 'my unmade bed sold for a fortune' woman, Sam, Damien, Jake and Dinos. No party is a wrap until the art pack shows up

Fluff Flick

No-brainer straight to DVD candyfloss movie aimed at Take A Break readers

GBH

Goody Bag Hell. Grabby celebs and grubby journos coming to blows over carriers containing £2k's worth of freebies at press launches and premieres is beyond ugly. Hopefully, it contains a diamante eye patch to cover the shiner that pushy fashion assistant just gave you.

Helloverload

We are fed up reading about nonebrities 'bravely coming to terms with their tragic loss' (i.e. broke a nail) or 'inviting us into their gracious city apartment' (rented by the hour from a location agent). Glossy tossy Hello!? Goodbye!

House
Squatting

Having promised ourselves 'never again!',
we're glued to the sofa and the Big Brother
inmates' mind-numbing existence
in that house

Hype Profile Celebrity

Overexposed red-carpet fixture that is
famous for what exactly? Step up Calum Best,
Flabi Titmuss, Tamara Beckwith, Fran
Cosgrave, Faria Alam, Rebecca Loos,
Lizzie from Wife Swap et al.

Irritainment

A hate-it-but-watch-it-anyway TV show. Anything
hosted by Jimmy Carr, Alan Carr, Mark Lamarr
or any other arrs

Ivy League

TV 'talent' that spreads out of control
like a persistent creeper: Davina, Dale,
Ant and Dec, Carole Smillie, Claire Sweeney,
Kate Thornton, Lorne Spicer and too many
others to name… somebody chop them
down please!

Jude The Obscure

Jude who? Wasn't he that blond one that
boffed the nanny and appeared in some dodgy
remake of a Michael Caine film, before getting
dumped by Sienna whassername?

Leprechaurny

Are there no TV stations in Ireland?
How come our screens are haunted
by pixie patter merchants full
of Leprechaurny blarney?
Shuffle off back to Shannon,
Gloria, Graham, Lil' Louis Walsh,
Patrick Kielty et al.

Madvert

A commercial so irritating it will drive you insane. Bev and Kev or Gimme Yop Me Mama should have public health warnings slapped on them

Marshmallow Movie

Soft, sweet, disposable, cinematic confection for a brain-disengage evening. Anything with Brittany Murphy or Ashton Kutcher should fit the bill

Media Smotherage

Press report overkill that leaves readers desperate for a breather from… election campaigns, The Ashes, Wimbledon, footballers' wives' beauty regimes, Chantelle's (who? we forgot already!) career, Sienna's new hairstyle. Suffocating!

Millionairhead

Paris Hilton, Nicole Richie,
Jade Goody et al.
Loaded and endearingly
daft as brushes

Mogadonna

What look is it this week, Mrs Ritchie?
English aristo, reformed slut. You're no longer
shocking, you tedious tranquilliser.
(Yawns and falls asleep)

Mossogyny

The Hate Kate brigade has been so cruel to La Moss.
It's impossible not to feel sympathy for a stunning,
pampered, multimillionairess… OK, maybe not

Nonebrity

A complete D-lister: hairdressers, models/actresses (whatever!), someone who had one line in Hollyoaks, Big Brother losers, etc. whose sole raison d'être is to fill voids in Hello! or OK!

Nontourage

The A-lister's ligging Nontourage of stylist, make-up artist, hairdresser, life coach, spiritual guru, dietary adviser and holistic therapist. Hun, that J.Lo and Mariah pose is so last century!

Number Crunchies

Dime-a-dozen little sweeties attractively packaged and useful for swelling the crowd at that PR bash, when A-listers are in short supply

Oprah Buffs

Advertising-industry term for a demographic that isn't necessarily after high art. humiliation on national TV at the hands of Trisha, Jeremy Kyle or Jerry Springer is more their thing… perfect for advertising your client's towelling trackie range to then

Osboured

Sharon and her 'oh please do share the minutiae of your glamorous lives with us everyday folks that are just like you' clan… N-ozzy 'atin!

Paunch and Judy

Media putdown to refer to any flaccid daytime-TV programme based on the Madeleys' format. Richard and his missus are untouchable icons. Accept no substitute!

Perma Ham

Irritating regular TV fixture who mugs outrageously to camera: David Dickinson and sundry hideous antiques 'experts', John McKrirrick, Russell Brand, Angus Deayton, Christine Hamilton, June Sarpong and Ainsley Harriett spring to mind

Plot Noodle

Junk TV fodder with preposterous
storylines. Desperate Housewives maybe?
Yet still we tuck into them. And as for that
spooky island plane crash survivors tosh…
totally Lost the Plot Noodle

Plum Jam

US Voguette Plum Sykes coins it in with
chick-lit hits Bergdorf Blondes and The
Debutante Divorcee. Have you read them?
More like Plum Duff! Jammy or what?

Poopscoopers

Paparazzi, showbiz and gossip
columnists – the lowest of the low.
They grub around in the latrines
of Z-list celebrity for an 'exclusive'.
But does anybody still give a toss?

Prada For Nada

Showering A-listers with freebie designer labels is a smart PR move. Nicole, Scarlett, Halle and Gwynnie are worthy Prada For Nada… And Abi Titmuss?… We'll take that as a 'no' then?

Red-Carpet Muncher

Shameless flashbulb junkie that attends any C-list opening, just to feed their publicity craving. Who are they? Open any issue of Hello!, you'll see

Siennemma

There are more gifted actresses,
her style is patchy and high streets are
swarming with better-looking women.
So why the endless diet of La Miller worship?
Frankly, she bores the shit out of us

Sofa Loafah

No cans, crisps, Corrie or Casualty for the
Sofa Loafah, the upmarket couch potato
favours Krug, caviar and property
shows featuring posh totty
Naomi Cleaver or Kirstie Allsopp

Soap Dodger

Why do we do it? Life is too short to
care about the events on the Street, the
Square or the Farm? Soap Dodgers avoid
the sofa and create some real-life dirty
storylines of their own

Soaporific

State of deep ennui wherein you collapse exhausted on the sofa and stare blankly at Emmerdale, Corrie and those whey-faced Walford whingers

Tr-ad-gedy

It's the celebrity ad campaign that is so annoying; target consumers decide to boycott the product. Hands up anyone who switched supermarket because of Sharon Osbourne, Prunella Scales or John Cleese?

Vernon Qué?

Exactly why is the scintillatingly witty, talented, Mancunian ex-model Mr Tess Daly never off our screens? Somebody… Anybody? No?

Wifestyle Coaching

Calling in the style gurus to sort out your other half's media image. Given some of the negative attention she attracts, Cherie Blair should report to the head of the queue

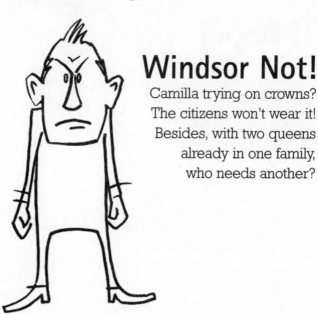

Windsor Not!

Camilla trying on crowns?
The citizens won't wear it!
Besides, with two queens
already in one family,
who needs another?

Zitcom

A 'comedy' aimed at pubescent popcorn munchers, preferably starring buff young Californians called Josh, Kyle and JayCee

Zzzzzelebrities

Just because you're on TV doesn't make you interesting, love. Could Kelly Brook or Kate Thornton be the cure for insomnia?

7

ON TREND

STYLE MATTERS

A Wristed Development

Enough with the ubiquitous charidee plastic bangles! You look like you're ready for the operating theatre. Good cause, bad look. We feel compassion fatigue kicking in

Arty Tack

A holographic print of a pickled sheep foetus? A vomit-stained 1960s duvet cover? A pile of empty bean cans on a bed of sculpted chewing gum? Having-a-laugh Hoxton galleries at heart-stopping prices. Massive Arty Tack

Bargain Debasement

Reduced to trawling the aisles of TK Maxx for last season's fashions? There's no stigma attached, darling, when even Vogue editors are at it too

Bargainista

'My jacket? £5 at Primark,' crows savvy Bargainista, leaving you to regret forking out £500 for an identical garment from Harrods

Bay Watch

Circling and hoping to spot a car pulling out of a parking bay with forty-five minutes left on the meter. Over the course of a year, this smart economic move will pay for a holiday in Antigua

Becksy

Putdown for an urban peacock. The nation's former favourite footballing big girl's blouse might look fit in an Alice band, you will just look like a silly wuss

Billy Butlin

Ridiculous holiday camp gear as seen on the Milan menswear catwalks. 'Pucci shirt, mules, tiger-print thong and Versace shades? Er, total Billy Butlin.'

Booking the Cooks

The new in-laws are due for dinner
and your sham cordon bleu credentials
risk being exposed. Cool cucumber, you call
in a posse of upmarket caterers and brazenly
pass the meal off as your own

Booteelicious

The fabulous frisson you get when you strut
your new £900 designer domanatrix
thigh-highs. To be worshipped is
your destiny, child!

Bow-Wow Wow-Factor

We'll be doggone. The US craze for blingy
canine couture has caught on here. Kit your
pooch in Pucci and Gucci for the ultimate
Bow-Wow Wow-Factor

Broke Black Mountain

Up to your eyeballs in debt, with a mound of identical dark clobber piled high in your wardrobe, yet you're contemplating adding to the heap by 'investing' in a £2k Dior number, because you 'need' it

Card Sharps

Smart money-makers switch credit cards every six months to take advantage of those 0% balance transfer offers. Cab to Selfridges please!

Cash strap trash crap

Not being judgemental, but, if you really can't afford the real thing and resort to market-stall designer rip-offs, expect no mercy

Chav Check

Not that you'd be caught dead in it, of course, but fake Burberry plaid is the give-away mark of the no-mark chav. Underclassy!

Channel Surfing

Upmarket booze cruises. The smart set has cottoned on to the fact that Chateau D'Yquem, Krug, Montecristos, foie gras and La Prairie all cost 50% less in Calais. No, we do not want a case of Le Piat D'Or, silly

Choo Fetish

When your budget says Dolcis, but your heart says Dolce G or Jimmy C killer heels, you got the Choo Fetish baby. Shoe-be-doo-be-doo

Chow Checker

Compulsive label-reading foodie saddo. Sat-fats calories and E numbers are Chow Checker hell. It's just a doughnut, you donut. Enjoy!

Condé Nasty

A fashion disaster, which may have looked funky on Karen Elson in Vogue, but which, in the real world, is a Frocky Horror Show. Knickerbockers, fishnets, wedges and Patagonian peasant top – somebody call the style police

Counter Espionage

Designer labels under constant surveillance?
Check! Location of must-have items identified?
Check! Shop assistants interrogated? Check!
Come 9am on day one of the sales, you're
going in and taking those babies out

Crapuccino

So your frothy coffee tastes of nothing? Too latte,
baby! Serves you right for frequenting those odious
high-street McMoccha chains

Cred
Shred

Cartoon socks and underpants?
Hide them from your latest squeeze or
risk total Cred Shred. Your reputation
will be in tatters

Crop Failure

**They look corny enough on beanpoles. But those
cut off at mid-calf trousers make you look like a
pumpkin. Bad case of Crop Failure**

Da Big Swoosh

Nike Town, Oxford Circus. The Saturday
meeting place of choice for any self-respecting
logo casual. Named after the brand's
trademark. As in: 'Sorted! Three at Da Big
Swoosh man, innit?'

Down Bagging

Leaving Gucci or Prada with that
expensive soft leather jacket switched
into a Lidl or Primark carrier
to avoid becoming a
mugger's target

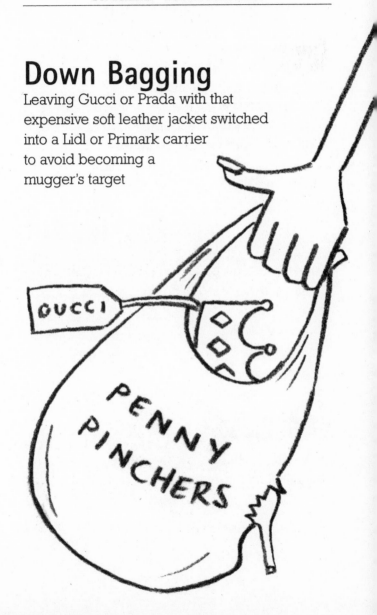

dot.common

While everyone buys online, we're back enjoying pukka personal service at a punter-free Knightsbridge superstore. Internet shopping is now tooo dot.common

EasyJet Set

Thanks to no-frills carriers, Riviera beaches resemble a bad day out in Blackpool. Smart money avoids the EasyJet Set preferring Montenegro to Monte Carlo

Embumpoint

Impressive bottom cleavage framed by designer hipster jeans. You've cracked it!

Esther

Apparently, Madonna prefers her adopted Kabbalah name, Esther. Let's hope fellow devotee Guy's alias ain't Polly. Polly & Esther? Material Girl Madgeness

Fallblack Option

Nothing in your wardrobe looks right for that big night out. Stick to your tried and tested Gucci little black dress – the perfect Fallblack Option

FASHBOS

The style police should hand out anti-fashion behaviour orders and ban Nancy Dell'Olio, Charlotte Church, Meg Matthews, Graham Norton and Jonathon Ross

not to be confused with

ASBro

The riot act you read when your younger sibling 'borrows' your D & G £300 strides and rips them at a student uni party. Get your dad to cut off his allowance (or sleep with his girlfriend, if you're really vindictive)

Fashion Faux Pash

Call the style police! There is no defence for the heinous crime of pashmina wearing. Hanging's too good for you

Flop Flip

One minute you are shuffling along, the next you are sent flying by those summer bendy beach sandals with minds of their own.
Oh Flop Flip!

Frockastocracy

Fashion royalty: US Vogue style queen
Anna Wintour and her court of camp
followers: Lee, John, Marc, Vivienne, Roland,
Giles, Stella, etc… but no trace of Florence
& Fred? The Emperor's New Clothes, surely?

Gastro Interioritis

The rush to turn every corner boozer into
formulaic gastropubs makes us queasy.
Edgy drinkers prefer the Dog & Duck
for its warm bitter, swirl carpet and a busty
barmaid called Brenda

Gastronomical

As prices rocket for some rocket-sprinkled signature dish in rip-off dining rooms, how long before they're exclusively populated by Elton John and Donald Trump? Reality (price) check please!

The Jitteratti

OD'd on espresso, talking twenty to the dozen, speeding out of your brain and shaking like a pneumatic drill operator. Welcome to The Jitteratti

Jock Frock

Phwoar! There's a horny-men-in-kilts revival going on. Jock Frocks rock! Euan McGregor looks well fit in one… although TV interior-design honcho John Amabile looks more like Mrs Doubtfire, sadly

Juicy Couture

Made-to measure, antioxidant-packed, wheatgrass, spirulina, ginger, carrot and apple smoothies are our Juicy Couture bespoke tip for a cold-free winter wardrobe

Knocked Back

That's scruffed up and dressed down to you. Fashionistas coo, 'That ripped Dries jacket, worn with 70s Osh Kosh dungaree shorts and Patagonian farmer's boots is so knocked back.' (NB not such a hot look on the knock kneed)

Logo Logic

Contemplating a divine but ruinously expensive Galliano coat, Logo Logic kicks in. I'll wear it forever (you won't). It goes with everything (it doesn't). And it's a true original (a high-street knockoff will be available any minute now). What the hell? It's only money

Logo Nogo

Dressing as a walking billboard for some global sportswear mega-brand is not clever – a total Logo Nogo

Maquill-ageing

Far from making you look ten years younger, the more you trowel on, the more you look like a painted dollop or one of those predatory dragons on your local department store's cosmetic counter. Slaphappy is so maquill-ageing

Molto Mañana

International fashionista speak for a hot trend that is beyond 'so now'. As in: 'Prints are so over, but black's coming back and looks Molto Mañana.

Net-à-porter

No need to endure those sniggering stick-insect 'assistants' as you emerge from the changing room like a sack of designer-bagged spuds, when you can get it all online these days. Net-à-porter, way to go'

Pong Pimp

Loo attendants who demand dosh for dousing
us in poncy 'parfum' get up our noses.
Do we look like we'd wear Joop?

Pushed

Pushed 'is the new 'edgy' in
fashionista speak. As in: 'That vintage
Ossie with the moon boots, ruff
and eye patch looks so pushed.'
(Trust us! It's a compliment)

Q List

Fashionista putdown for mere mortals
suffering the indignity of an in-store waiting
list for this season's must have designer
essentials. As in: 'Darling, those
Nat Mag girls are so Q-list.'

Scissor Sister Bliss

Who cares whether your radically restyled barnet is
by Nicky Clarke or Nikki of Carlisle. So long as it cuts
it, you're in Scissor Sister Bliss

Skibegeebees

In your Dior salopette, you're finally part of the St Moritz scene, but, faced with that deadly downhill vertical slalom, suddenly you're not so sure. Bad case of the Skibegeebees!

not to be confused with

eBaygeebees

That vintage Zandra Rhodes poncho you bought for £300 looks ludicrous and the 'designer' fragrance smells of wee. eBaygeebees

Traumaties

Acid trip Paisley pattern, 'witty' cartoons,
Van Gogh's Sunflowers or worn with matching
shirt à la Chris Tarrant… those Traumaties are
seriously disturbing, pain-in-the-neck-wear

Trinnie Trannie

Wardrobe crisis? Put yourself in the hands of a
personal shopper and you too can drag up like
some boring What Not To Wear clone. Style
guru? Surrey, Susannah… you're so suburban!

Turnup Downer

The inevitable consequence of wearing your retro denims down to the floor is that you catch your shoe in 'em and fall over. Turnup Downer!

Ultradoshy

Fashionista speak for very expensive.
As in: 'I'm on the waiting list for
the new YSL tote bag.
Ultradoshy, but, then,
investment dressing
doesn't come cheap!'

Vintage Plonkers

Fashion freaks spending small fortunes on glammy 'vintage'. Dynasty shoulder pads and Dallas sequins? More like Anita Dobson or Cilla circa 1984

The Von Trap

Those Von Dutch rock-chick T-shirts are looking a tad Eurotrashy. VD is not a good look

Waistbanned

Designer underwear showing above your kecks is pure pikey pants! This logo nogo should be Waistbanned immediately

as should

Whale Tails

Noticed how the triangular backs to thongs poking above your jeans look like Whale Tails? Not as nasty as camel hoof, but still one to avoid

Wig Whammy

Your expensive lopsided mullet cut looks like Friar Tuck meets Pocahontas. You've been scalped petal – a bad Wig Whammy

Zara Fillips

Out on your lunch break, you check out everyone's fave Spanish clothiers and discover that 'Prada' skirt you've been lusting after in Vogue. At a mere £29, your right royal snip is a stylish Zara Fillip

8

ON THE LASH

NO MORE THAN 21 UNITS FOR WOMEN AND 28 FOR MEN PER WEEK, MIND YOU!

ABC

Anything But Chardonnay.
Simply no one is drinking it any more

Barf Lies

'I'll never drink again!'
you moan, as your mate watches
you throw up a night's booze in the loos.
Yeah! Barf Lies!

Beer Overcoat

After ten pints of Belgian brew, it's amazing how we will happily wander the streets in a short-sleeved T-shirt even when it's minus six degrees. Must be the Beer Overcoat

Blue Sky Thinking

Ad agency brainstorming session where you're encouraged to think out of the box

to be followed at 6pm prompt by a spot of

Blue Sky Drinking

Ad-agency-speak for a brain-damaging session. We too have been known to come up with some brill ideas when we've drunk ourselves out of the box

Cold Crawling

You finally come to and begin to wonder if last night's alcohol-induced indiscretion has landed you in the doghouse. Time to pick up the phone and do some serious Cold Crawling

Craic Den

A great Irish pub, a few barrels of the black stuff, bizarre conversations about keeping horses in your home, Sean Keane and Seamus Donnelly on the jukebox and some old biddy offering to read your palm... we're hooked!

Dishevelled

Trashed, wrecked, trollied,
steaming, blootered, paralytic...
all sound so uncouth. The elegantly
wasted prefer 'Dishevelled'.
Drunk as a skunk in a stylish way

Donna Kebab

Sauced-up disco dolly. Avoid! Avoid! She'll demand
a Turkish takeaway then throw up over your
Gucci jacket in the back of the cab

Dyssentrested

Off your food big time and
trapped on the john? OK, you
were bladdered, but we did tell
you not to sample a frankfurter and
onions from that greasy street-hawker's
cart last night. Hot dog? Presumably!

E.biza Tan

White-as-a-sheet new arrival at Manchester
Airport. After two weeks of luvved-up clubbing
(and sleeping all day) in San Antonio, they're
sporting the E.biza Tan

FUDs

Fookin' ugly drunks. Leave the club half an hour before closing time. Being picked up by the FUDs is too depressing

The Furstenberg Fairy

After five pints of her delicious brew, the fabulous Furstenberg Fairy magically turns Dave from Dispatch into Brad Pitt… then back to Jabba the Hut by the time you wake up in his pit the next morning

Gutter Surfing

Out on the town, caning it large
and now you're in fall-down-drunk mode.
Welcome to the weekend world of
Gutter Surfing!

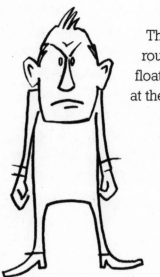

Hovercrafty

They hang around when a
round's being ordered, but
float off when it's their shout
at the bar. Hovercrafty devils

Jellied Heels

The worse-for-wear party monsters rolling around city centres and wobbling on four-inch spikes. Not such (Jade) Goody Choo Shoes

Kate Moshed

New slang term meaning 'to be in a bit of a state'. A high flier exhibiting less than model behaviour. Talk about messy missy

Lateral Drinking

Out on the lash and with the bar set to close in twenty minutes you rapidly line them up. Four pints in a row to be downed. Serious Lateral Drinking

Magic Taxi

Bladdered to the point of
forgetting where you live,
you somehow make it back in
one piece. 'The Magic Taxi got
me home again last night.'

Malibu Mermaid

Bartender-speak for blonde bimbettes out to
lure unsuspecting lads to a terrible fate: paying
for a kebab and a taxi back to hers, before
being chucked out and left all at sea – broke
and five miles from home

Mike Dyson

Ferocious drunk
who hoovers up everything
in sight before depositing his
contents on the floor

Mocktail

Alcohol-free cocktails are the healthy option. Try The Sadie: frothy designer bitter lemon in a frosted glass

Muntered

Mashed up and looking like a heaving minger. As in: 'We drank so much, we ended up totally Muntered.'

Nasty Spumante

It's a fast track to the hangover from hell.
We don't care that it's on a special offer at £3.99
for two bottles: cheap fizz is a swizz so give us
the bizz! Ruinart or Mumm will do nicely

Pastis Sell-By Date

Sad but true. While the summer aniseed aperitif
slips down a treat on balmy Riviera quaysides,
on a wet night in Blighty, it's less les couilles du
chien more le oui du chat

Pishydishy

After sixteen Sea Breezes, Rancid Rod
from Rotherham becomes strangely sexy.
Negative! Through heavy beer goggles,
even Johnny Vegas looks Pishydishy

Pomagne Brain

A shrieking gaggle of silly, sozzled, suburban Sharons
out on the pull? Bunch of Pomagne Brains!
More dizzy than fizzy!

Prole Dancers

Chavvy Tango-tan trailer
trash tanking up at your local nightspot
on buy-one-get-three-free alcopops. Avoid!

Ropey Dopey

Hungover again and looking dog rough.
You can barely string two words together
when you're feeling this Ropey Dopey

Rosédozy

Ah! Here comes summer! Long languid
evenings, grabbing some rays and getting
Rosédozy on chilled Côtes de Provence?
Bring it on!

Sauvignon Blank

It started as 'a quick glass of wine after work'
and ended up as another 'can't remember
getting home last night'. A total Sauvignon
Blank then?

Savoy Cabbaged

Upmarket drunk... totally brain dead after two too many Martinis in a very posh cocktail lounge

Slurry Blurries

After litres of alcopop, you're babbling like a baboon and your vision's turned swimmy – bad case of the Slurry Blurries

A Stiff Kick in'

Call us Martini masochists, but
we love the sensation of a well-heeled
cocktail putting the boot in

Teahab

Where you should be headed at this rate.
Packed with antioxidants and polyphenols,
white- and green-leaf brews are the hot drink
du jour. Check in to Teahab and check out your
newly glowing skin… and, no, a green tea
Martini does not count!

Tightmare

Late for that first date or interview and, as you slide out of the cab, you realise those new £30 10 deniers have more ladders than the Fire Brigade. Tightmare!

not to be confused with

Tight Mare

Bar lush who accepts your hospitality all night but is so mean they wouldn't dream of giving you the steam off their piss in return

Tikkataboo

You won't be if you visit that dodgy all-night Balti house. No matter how hammered and hungry you may be, avoid that Delhi Belly shack and hit the sack instead

similarly

Traj Mahal

Off your trolley at the Tandoori, you gorge
yourself on poppadoms and red-hot curry,
washed down by four pints of lager, before
chucking the whole lot up vin-da-loo. Traj!

Toasted

**Hot? Burned out? Crispy? Frazzled? It's the
hangover from hell as you got Toasted last night
and spent all your bread. Aw, poor flour!
Fail to make it in to work by ten though
and you really will be toast**

Too Slurred With Love

You've fancied him for weeks but, when you try
your carefully rehearsed chat-up line, it comes
out as tongue-tied, jabbering jumble. You're Too
Slurred With Love, love. What a Lulu!

Va Va Voom Vacuum

Deadly dull party?
Less fun than a wet
weekend in Walthamstow?
It's a Va Va Voom Vacuum.
So Hoover up the hooch, sweep
the buffet and leg it pronto!

9

KIDDING ON

IT'S A FAMILY AFFAIR

Au Pairanoia

The twenty-year-old leggy Latvian live-in seemed like the solution to your baby-bound existence. Now your man's staying in to 'fix the car' (again), while suggesting you go out with the girls. You're beyond suspicious, in the grip of rampant Au Pairanoia

Baby Bio

When asked how your sprog is, 'fine, thanks' is all we require. Breast v bottle, teething problems, first words, family resemblances? We don't do details. Spare us the Baby Bio!

Baby Sham

Toddlers' tea party as cover for mums to get tanked up on cheap bubbly in the afternoon

Backseat Mother

Your mother, a first-time gran, now imagines she's needed to dole out unwanted advice 24/7 on how to raise your baby. Given the job she did on you, you're not exactly listening

Baggage Handling

Dealing with the tiresome demands of an ex-partner. 'Can't do Saturday. Gotta take the kids out and do a spot of Baggage Handling.'

Beach Buggy

They splatter you with sand, whine for ice cream, knock your drinks over with their ball, then trip and pour a pail of water over your Liza Bruce cossie... Is there any EU law against strapping other people's kids to a surfboard and shoving them out to sea?

Bottigelli

The lotions and potions you lovingly rub into your little oil painting of a cherub's nappy-rashy tush

Brat Pack

Ringing his mum, you claim, 'The kids are pleading to stay with you for the weekend.' Bribing them with carte blanche at Toys R Us, you Brat Pack them off and snatch forty-eight hours of self-indulgent bliss

Clockwork Orange

Have you wondered why your child is so prone to 'losing' their pay-as-you-go mobiles? Poor love is being tormented at school because you keep buying them Clockwork Oranges. Nokia clever move really, is it?

Dad Nauseam

Those old chestnuts your father trots out with monotonous regularity whenever he has an audience. Like we need to hear what you and the lads got up to in Benidorm in 1976 again!

Déjà Poo

We warned you. Babies are hard work.
When you're on the fourteenth nappy
change of your Groundhog Day, it all
starts to seem a bit Déjà Poo

Derangels

Wicked! Just before they are due for beddy
byes, we force feed them sweets. Up all night
running around while off their faces on E
numbers? Serves you right for letting your
precious brats sick up on our new Paul Smith
jacket

Fourbies

School-run mums in oversized 4x4s. Toughen your wimpy imps up by making them use public transport … and stop clogging up our streets!

Hipster Genes

This genetic-tampering lark is getting scary. Are we about to spawn a whole generation of Gucci-obsessed, body-perfect, hyper-smart Stepford Children?

Holiday Snap Trap

Luring you round for drinks only to corner you with 300 variations on the 'This is us with the children outside the hotel' theme is just not on. Taxi!

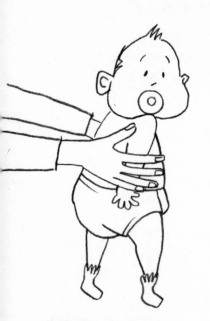

Hyperdiaper

Poo poo any invitation to babysit your mate's sprog until it's properly potty trained. You'll regret your largesse when you're changing little Hyperdiaper's third nappy in an hour

Kidology

Parental one-upmanship. Bigging up your precocious brat's incredible talents and exceptionally high IQ, you say Tarquin's taken to Tolstoy. We know he's not over Teletubbies

Party Bag Slag

Collecting junior from the new neighbours' kid's birthday do, you and a friend inspect the contents of the party bag he was handed, bitching about how its tacky contents confirm the latest occupants of number 18 are just too common for words

Paternity Suit

Hurrah, she's pregnant! Play her at her own game for once and splash out on that £1,500 whistle you clocked at Ozwald Boateng. 'It'll come in handy for the christening, darling.'

Posh Splice

Nowt to do with that skinny Beckham woman, we're talking pukka wedding, usually held at the ancestral seat, where the new couple become Lord and Lady Sebag-Farquahar-Tompkinson-Smythe. The guests' tiaras would blow off if they knew fat Ffion was actually three months in the Ffamily way though

Pregnant Applause

Just because you managed to get yourself up the duff, we're supposed to stand around and cheer?

Pramateur Dramatics

In their 4x4-sized buggies, dummy-spitting, rattle-chucking, show-off, designer-clad sprogs act up big time, while their blinkered parents expect you to drool, 'Aaah, cute!' Listen up, squirts, I'm the star around here!

Resigoo

The sticky mess your sprog regurgitates back on to his bib. It's putting us off our risotto

Rugratrun

Mums in tacky trackies offloading kids at the school gates. 'Let's do coffee after the Rugratrun.'

Scummy Mummy

Yummy mummy, you? Rolling in trollied from the pub with another new 'uncle' in tow, not even noticing your kid is watching your porn DVD, then emptying their piggy bank to buy a pack of Silk Cut from the garage across the road and telling them they might as well find out now that their dad is a bastard? Joan Crawford had nothing on you, Scummy Mummy Dearest

Shower Cap

A mutually agreed upper
spending limit on gifts
for that ubiquitous American
import, the baby shower

classier than the

Power Shower

Blatant jockeying for Godmother status, as
rivals attempt to outdo one another by
lavishing ridiculously expensive gifts on
the imminent arrival. An entire wardrobe of
Gucci-Gucci-goo for example

S.I.T.C.O.M.

Single Income, Two Children, Outrageous
Mortgage. Think twice before one of you quits
the rat race. Stay-at-home parenting is no
domestic comedy

The Sitter Jitters

New mum on a rare night out? Stop ringing
home every ten minutes to check up on junior.
Like the babysitter is going to flog the
sprog on eBay? Chill, hun!

Sprog-A-Jog (aka Buggers)

Aerobic workout favoured by fanatical keep-fit parents, who pound the pavements at breakneck speed, with bemused brat strapped into those three-wheeler buggies turned jogging frames

Yelly Babies

Is hearing loss a side-effect of parenthood? Your screaming tots are overrunning restaurants, cafes and public transport, yet somehow you remain oblivious to the racket. Yelly Babies suck, sweetie

10

ON YOUR NERVES

LIFE SUCKS

1-1-HATE

Your directory enquiry routes via Delhi.
You ask for Selfridges and get a local Hotpoint
dealer's number (they sell fridges, don't they?).
Pure 1-1-Hate! And we thought 192 sucked?

629ers

London congestion charge zone avoiders
petrified of copping a ten-seconds-too-soon
£60 penalty before Night-Mayor Ken's highway
robbery clocks off at half past six. We can't get
along the Marylebone Road for 629ers

Aisle Rage

Supermarket psychologists, take note! Repositioning the salt, sugar and eggs every five weeks so we'll grab their impulse-buy replacements just makes us get wild in the aisles and confirms you as money-grabbing manipulators. Support your local corner shop while you still can!

Appro Pro

Professional party queen, who'll 'borrow' a £500 frock from a department store, wear it once then get a refund. Spill Campari over her and watch that smug grin curdle

Artburn

At the local gallery's private view, the combination of indigestible avant-garde 'sure to be a Turner Prize nominee' pretence and cheap white gut-rot wine is enough to give you a bad case of Artburn

Balance Slip–Up

'Surely there's a zero missing here?' you wail, as the ATM receipt impudently points out that you're down to your last fifty quid with ten days left before payday

Battenberg

Holidaymaker (inevitably British) who has sunbathed in different-shaped tops and bottoms of varying lengths on alternate days, hence, the skin attractively sectioned into pink, tan and white squares like the cake of the same name

Being Gobbled

Student-speak for stony broke. Stems from ATMs that swallow up your cash card when your limit is exceeded. As in: 'Can't buy you a pint, mate, I've just Been Gobbled.'

Bloatograph

You pose seductively to camera, imagining yourself as Elle McPherson, but what prints out looks more like Demis Roussos. Bloatograph!

Call Centremental

Navigating through multiple-option menus, then being held for fifteen minutes in piped-music hell, before being harassed by a barely intelligible drone in some far-flung land is driving us Call Centremental and making us increasingly sentimental for old-fashioned operators 'connecting you now'

Cam Dram

Doing 40 in a 30 zone, you clock the telltale flash in your mirror. Just three points away from disqualification, you'll now have to sweat it out. Hideous Cam Dram

Camel Hoof

The nastiest form of front VPL. 'What was she thinking of? Did you see the Camel Hoof those lycra ski pants gave her?'

Camera Shysters

Fast-buck jokers trying to flog you gadgets like swivel number plates or dazzle spray to beat the universally hated revenue-raiser ubiquitous speed cams

Carisma Bypass

Fifty-three, balding, paunchy, dressed like Noel Edmonds? Don't imagine driving a scarlet Lamborghini or similar spendy wheels makes you cool, sexy or interesting. Carisma Bypass

Chavisty of Justice

Some skanky scally on the rob trips over a loose paving stone on your path as he makes off with the contents of your house. He's handed twenty minutes' community service and his brief sues you for six grand for the damages he's sustained. Total Chavisty of Justice

Chavrolet

Blacked-out windows, blue lights under its skirts, ear-shattering exhaust, hip hop that can be heard six miles away, go-faster stripes and posse of tanked-up Tiffanys and Jades as passengers: the essential components of a customised Chavrolet

Checkout Charlie

At the express till, the jester in front pays for his milk and Hobnobs by Visa. We're in a hurry, so flash the cash, you Checkout Charlie!

Chelsea Tractor (Aka the 4x4)

Narrow city streets were not designed for these cumbersome brutes. Chiswick, Bearsden and Solihull are as deep into the countryside as these pathetic poseurs will ever venture

Ciggy Liggy

Annoying bar-room cadger. Please stop asking to 'borrow' a fag. Those coffin nails cost 25p each and we're not feeling charitable. Puff off!

also known as

Tab Hunter

Forced on to the street for a mid-morning snout, you're assailed by an army of professional Tab Hunters. No, we can't 'lend' you a fag, you matinee idler

Con-Fusion

Restaurants serving culinary hybrids: Indo-Italian tapas served with chopsticks, Pacific Rim Nouvelle; Sizchuan-Tex-Mex mezze in a bento box. Farcical fusion food pretence at rip-off prices. Cookery crass

Cycle-Pathic Behaviour

Two-wheeler Lycra louts hell bent on taking you out for daring to stray, daydreaming, into their precious bike lane. Retaliate by puncturing a tyre with a penknife. Now tri-cycle on that!

Dagenham

Mad, crazy, loony, howling, bonkers?
That wild child is pure Dagenham… that is,
five stops beyond Barking

DEALINQUENTS

Agreeing to buy something and then haggling for discount and free stuff to be thrown in is not savvy negotiation, merely bad form. You're in Basingstoke not a basement souk!

Delhi Selly

You're engrossed in the must-see TV moment of all time when some unintelligible Indian call-centre clown rings with some cheap gas, free mobile or home-improvement scam. Spare us the Mumbai Jumbo!

Dishcloth Diva

What's with all this compulsive surface wiping? Your flatmate/partner has suddenly gone from grungy slacker to obsessive Dishcloth Diva. We're blaming Kim and Aggie

dot.con

An online scam. You thought you were confirming your security details with your bank. In reality, you just paid for a whole family of scallies' fortnight in Majorca

Eary Silence

A call-centre computer dials you at random but the salesman picks up another line leaving you with an annoying and spookily Eary Silence

Edinbores

Irritating Festival media pseuds, who drone on smugly about the significance of some turgid Scandinavian two-hander they 'discovered' in a draughty church hall in Leith

Energy Vampire

Your egocentric mate's idea of a night out involves a three-hour 'me me me' monologue, which leaves you utterly drained.
Self-obsessed Energy Vampires suck

Enders

Nowt to do with the Beeb's dire soap, but every bit as annoying. People who insist on punctuating their conversation with 'at the end of the day'. More common than muck

Eye Cholesterol

Something so visually offensive as to be potentially damaging to your health. As in: 'Went to Blackpool. Some of the sights in swimsuits... serious Eye Cholesterol.'

Fixed Penalty Shoot-Out

Unfairly ticketed by traffic wardens? Always take it to extra time by challenging the heartless sods in court. You'd be surprised at how often you'll get a result

Flop Strop

Your girlfriend having a pop at you on account of some turkey you dragged her to see at the theatre or cinema. 'I didn't direct the bleedin' movie!' you hiss, while she throws a Flop Strop... and, by the way, two tickets, drinks and popcorn comes to more than the average Ecuadorian's annual wage, you ungrateful cow

Geriatric Furrow

Stuck-in-a-groove story that didn't remotely interest you the first time around. 'Did I tell you about Elsie at number 7's hip operation?' 'Yes, dear!' Then she ploughs on regardless

Gym Jam

You pay 25 million quid a year in fees but at 7pm you can't find an available piece of equipment at your private health club. A personal trainer and a home gymnasium for you then?

Habitual Bitches

Annoying smug girlfriends who boast about how they've kicked their habits, just as you succumb to another Marlboro Light while ordering a Danish with your grande cappuccino

Hairmoanal

It's that time of the month. Fresh from the salon and barely two minutes through the door, she's whinging that it's 'too short, too blonde, too fluffy, too common'. Gordon Barnet!

similarly

Hair Rage

'I said I wanted to look like Erin O'Connor not Des O'Connor!' you fume, flying off the handle, hacked off with the hacked-off bob the silly crimper has landed you with. Fasten your safety belt; it's going to be a bumpy ride!

Intellectual Sequins

Trendy 'intellectual' reading matter, strategically scattered around your pad, to show you're bang on the zeitgeist, Jonathan Franzen, Michel Houellebecq, etc. While in reality, you found Bridget Jones' Diary a bit of a stretch

Irritable Towel Syndrome

Having headed off to the sun, you hit poolside at 9am, only to discover those pesky Germans have put their markers down on every available lounger. Aaagh! Irritable Towel Syndrome

ISAdermy

The state of being stuffed by financial advisers who convince you to plough your annual tax-free allowance into equities two days before world markets crash

Lastminute.bom

A dud gig you hurriedly booked over the net without researching it. A week in a fetid Faliraki flophouse, front-stalls tickets to see some Pop Idol loser, twin cabins on a luxury liner named Poseidon

Leaning Tower of Visa

When those post-Christmas bills
and credit card statements
flood in, you'll pile 'em
high and panic about
your Leaning
Tower of Visa

Londonitis

A virulent social disease characterised by feverish ranting about house prices, school catchment areas, members-only nightclubs, hot new restaurants, celebrity diets and designer labels. It's catching!

M4 Bores

Self-satisfied social-climber couples who 'don't do weekends', as they'll be down at the new country 'hice' in some dreary hamlet west of Swindon. (Green wellie) M4 Bores!

Mind the Gap

Inconsiderate fellow tube user who invades your space with legs splayed akimbo at 90 degrees. Mind the Gap, mate!

Mrs Kipling

Avoid this fruitcake like the plague. Body swerve the barking mad biddy before she pins you down at the village fete or church social. 'More tea, vicar?'

Mugshot Mugging

Shoving your camera phone in our dials when we least expect it, then sending your mates pics of us as moonfaced freaks plain isn't funny, you minging Mugshot Mugger

Muscle Sprouts

Pumped-up gymsters with all the personality of a flatulence-inducing vegetable. Nothing like Muscles from Brussels, Jean-Claude Van Damme, then?

Naussies

Annoying antipodean backpackers. They nick all our jobs and moan ad nauseam about the weather, transport, housing costs, how much better Sydney is, etc. Whinging Poms have nothing on this lot!

No-Mark Names

Mini-Chav monikers are a hoot: Shamian, Shantell, Diadora, Denim, Paris-Brittany, Cortez, Arizona Storm. But the Beckhams do it best. Talk about a Cruz to bear in later life!

Pandemonium

You come back from a relaxing weekend away to find all your housemates' dirty pots stacked high in the sink. Pandemonium! Shame you don't share with a bunch of scrubbers

Phisy Chips

Scammed credit cards based on information
you give out to cod websites. Watch your
account take a battering

Phoney Friend

8.45pm. You take a call. 'Congratulations,
you've won a luxury cruise to the Bahamas,'
chirrups the pre-recorded Swiss Tony voice.
It's your Phoney Friend again. Don't even
think about calling back on that £25-a-minute
'prize line' number, you sucker

Pijslapped

Splat! Your brand-new navy
coat just got happy slapped
from on high by vermin on the
wing. Trafalgar Square?
Not an option!

Pin Code Overload

With a dozen bits of plastic, your mind's a blank at the cash point. Birthdays, anniversaries, last time Spurs won the cup? Whatever numbers you perm, it's Pin Code Overload

Pin Prick

Being held up at the hole-in-the-wall by some loser who can't remember four simple numbers. It's not rocket science, you Pin Prick

PL8 H8

We've spotted SUC8, MA551V and SEK51. But personalised number plates are just 22 SAD. Guess who drives V2 8ONO? Enough said

Post Traumatic Stress Syndrome

The postie calls when you're in the shower, leaving you with an advice note and a two-mile hike in the rain to the sorting office, where, after a twenty-minute wait, a surly youth hands over a recorded-delivery envelope containing a final demand for that £300 you owe

Quiet Coaching

They sit in the only no-mobiles carriage on a long train journey and proceed to take call after loud call. Give them a bit of strong but Quiet Coaching and, if they persist, get the train manager (that's the new term for guard apparently) to chuck 'em off at Doncaster

The Rage of Chivalry

You wave a driver out in front of you and they sneer at you for being a wimp. You hold a door open for a woman who sails past with her nose in the air. There's a bad-manners pandemic out there and the Rage of Chivalry is upon us

Red Dread

Final reminders can ruin a potentially blissful day; so never check the mail before you go out. Why let the Red Dread stop you from seeing the world through rose-tinteds

Rollover Crackpot

Can't get near the till for them. Odds on landing the Lotto jacky are the same as a decent Guy and Madonna movie – about 14 million to one. Save your money, you Rollover Crackpot, and stop boring us with how you'll spend it

Round the Bendy

Those hateful, double-length, joined-up buses clogging every road junction are impossible to manoeuvre past. Talk about driving us Round the Bendy

Scent to Coventry

Doused yourself in knockoff designer pong and now nobody will come near you? You've been Scent to Coventry, you cheap stinker

alternatively

Seriously Rongpong!

Olfactory senses overpowered by your neighbour's offensive designer perfume, you turn to her and sneer, 'Seriously Rongpong, sweetie!' Thierry Mugler's Angel gets right up our noses

Script Tease

The call-centre operator or the cheesy waiter launch into their deeply annoying rehearsed spiel. Wind them up by lobbing in a random unrelated question and hear their robotic sales pitch fall apart

Scum Shuttle

Off-peak bargain-basement internal flight where you are crammed in like cattle and treated like deportees by vile crones in lurid uniforms

Stepford Street

Mega-brands are forcing independent traders out of high streets, creating clone-zone shopping ennui. 'Fancy some retail therapy in Reading? Nah, pure Stepford Street.'

Stroppy Shoppy

Luxury-goods emporium whose paid-buttons assistants still think condescension is the new black. Demand complimentary tea and champagne, then haggle like you're in a Cairo souk, just to annoy the smug dimwits

Supplement Overdose

No, we're not talking too much Vit C. It's those damned weekend pullout sections mounting up unread in the corner and making us feel slightly anxious. Bin 'em and say good riddance to troublesome piles

Tobleroad

Local councils have turned our streets
into alpine assault courses resembling a
famous Swiss choccie bar. It's giving
us the speed-bump hump

Terminal Boredom

Your flight to Paris is delayed due to 'an operational problem'. Tedious or what? You flick through Heat (again), wind up easyJet staff (doesn't everyone?), laugh at the style casualties boarding for Ibiza… anything to relieve the Terminal Boredom.
Take the Eurostar next time!

Toxic Sock Syndrome

No matter how carefully you sort the laundry, a rogue sock infects the Zanussi, turning pristine whites a fetching shade of sky blue. Panic, then dash to Tesco for a sachet of Colour Run

Trolleywood Babylon

Must-to-avoid rush-hour hell of the local superstore. 'Sainsburys? Saturday? At seven? Are you insane? Trolleywood Babylon, sweet pea.'

Veneereal Disease

There may well be entire TV channels devoted to them, but brush-on teeth whiteners are never socially acceptable. You look like Red Rum, chum

Vintage Whine

The '62 Margaux? Frankly, we doubt whether you could tell the difference between that and Lambrusco, you Vintage Whine snob

Web Spinners

Chat-room daters who
reinvent themselves by
lying outrageously about
their looks, age, career, income, etc.

Wrap Flap & Rip Rage

Impossible-to-open CDs, milk cartons, jiffy
bags, parcels, etc. put us in a wrap flap. Tearing
at them in a rip rage frenzy always ends with a
broken nail. Use the Scissors Sister!

11

ON THE TURN

IN THE PINK

Bareback Mounting

Bug chasing is never clever. Rubber up before you climb in the saddle! Welcome to condom country, cowboy!

Benderbender

A heavy weekend booze and cruise session. From knocking-off time on Friday until you crawl out of some sleazy sauna at eight o'clock on Monday morning

Canapé

A bit of a slapper. A tasty dish that's viewed as finger food. As in: 'Dale's been putting himself around a bit lately, pure Canapé.'

Costa Packet

Sitges, the gay beach capital of Spain. And when they hit the playa, it's not the prices they are bitching about, more what those hunks are toting in their trunks (See Pantyhose)

Czech Mates

Eastern European porn movies with unintelligible plots, but lots of cute queens to stroke your bishop to on a lonely knight

Dicksy Chick

Go, cowboy! You are finally making out with the smokin' Dolly Parton lookalike you've been chatting up all night. Your hand slides slowly up her firm thighs… and cops a surprise package that really ought not to be there. Balls! It's a ladyboy… that's so not country!

Doing the Gay Gardens

No, it's not a Scottish dance. Doing the Gay Gardens involves exotic blooms, precious petals, delicate flowers and neatly trimmed bushes… and a body double for that topless hoer from Desperate Housewives planting seeds

Dorian Gay

Buff fifty-five-year-olds in Evisu and Duffer and still larging it on the scene. Growing old disgracefully? Why the hell not?

Duracell Bunnies

As in: 'at it like…' They go on and on and on and on like randy rabbits

Dykotomy

Unable to decide whether to come out on the side of tipping the velvet or snogging the snake

not to be confused with

Dyechotomy

Panic! Your attempt at Davina McCall auburn has left you looking like Dame Edna Everage. Should you go back to blonde and risk it turning green or invest in a Hermes scarf, therein lies the Dyechotomy

e.number

Someone you pulled on the web and have been mailing re a hot date. 'Logged on to Gaydar, m8, and found myself a cute e.number for the weekend!'

Fairy Lite

Straight boys obsessing about their appearances, back, sack and crack waxes, eyebrow tweezing and generally acting camper than a Chelsea Flower Show tent. Is there something in the water?

also

Fauxmosexual

Why are all the hunkiest straight men acting a tad gay? 'Cos girlies are bored with loutish lads and prefer a sweet, well-turned-out, gym-toned, designer-labelled Fauxmo. Get in touch with your feminine side

Fruitballer

The macho world of soccer
is notoriously homophobic, but
it's common knowledge that the
Premiership contains several star
players who would like to shoot and
score for the other team... and not
necessarily in that order

Fruit Looping

Cruising the gay scene. Have a banana, lose
your cherry and go home with a pear!
They're all ripe for the picking

The Gaybours

Aka Bryan and Ryan, the sweet couple that just moved in next door. But be very worried when you're out of town and they invite your hunky bloke round for a 'Sunday roast'

Gaydar Years

The net nancy's fave online dating site is full of old dogs posing as young pups. Sixty-four? That'll be twenty-three in Gaydar Years then

Gayhem

Brett, your hairdresser, is in tears. Brian the boyf just dumped him for his personal trainer Baz, who lives with his ex Brad – the one who stole all his Kylie CDs, went to Brazil and came back as Brandy. Worst of all, he's spilled purple tint on his new D & G crop top. Utter Gayhem!

Inky
Twinky

Muscle Mary sporting those
ubiquitous ink-blue Celtic armband
tattoos. Send in the clones!

Manscaping

It started on the gay scene. Now all male
peacocks are increasingly resorting to the
knife. Six-pack sculpting and pecs implants are
the fastest-growing Manscaping procedures

Mildred Pierced

Would-be butch bloke with a mugful of metal
studs and pins and a tonne of body piercings.
Closet Joan Crawford fan more like

Narnia

**As in: 'Tom's so far in the closet he's in Narnia.'
No fairytale ending then?**

Pete Burns Victim

The Dead Or Alive front man is a style icon and true original. Your attempt at alternative drag looks like you raided Vanessa Feltz's closet and had your slap done by Jodie Marsh... or Dawn Davenport from John Waters's Female Trouble

Pantyhose

The boys' favourite beach pastime is checking out those Speedo bulges. 'Clock the Pantyhose on that, girlfriend!'

Paxo

Newsnight anchor? No! Just a good stuffing …
but make sure that chicken's old enough to
take it up the Gary

(as in)

GARY GLITTER

Cockney rhyming slang for…

Pink Pounder

A stud muffin. Just what a lucky lad wants between his buns. Comes with relish usually

Rag Hag

Someone you trail along in your wake for company, safe in the knowledge that her deeply questionable fashion sense is unlikely ever to leave you sartorially upstaged

'Roid Rage

Unpredictable aggressive outbursts from vicious, pumped-up gym queens that have popped far too many steroid pills

Sapphisfaction
The state of loving your inner lesbian

Taxidermy
As the cab pulls up outside
your place, you realise you must
have dropped your wallet and can't
pay. You're stuffed! At least you hope you will
be, as you ask the mega-cute cabbie whether
there's anything you can do for him by
way of a favour

Tina Turner
Disco diva off his tits and private dancing on
Crystal Meth (aka Tina... it's a VERY BAD habit)

Triga Happy

Being chuffed to have a copy of the latest
saucy-action DVD featuring dirty Brit scallies
up to no good. Cocks his pistol, pulls
Triga and shoots

Viagra Falls

It's the most fashionable stimulant on the scene…
cue thunderous cascading torrents

Vim Diesel

An abrasive muscular butch lesbian
that's a bit of a scrubber

12

ON THE LIPS, ON THE HIPS

PILING IT ON

Ab Flab

Sweetie, if you plan to wear a crop top this summer, now is the time to get that Ab Flab into the nearest gym... or adopt the Patsy Stone diet

Atkins Dragons

The Atkins diet can make your mouth smell less than fresh. Go breathe your fetid fumes over someone else, honey!

Bad Hangover

The New Year's fitness resolution has worn off. With cocktails and takeaways back on the menu, your waist is spilling out of your Top Shop hipster jeans. Oh dear, Bad Hangover

Belly Bunter

Teletubby-proportioned bint who thinks bumster jeans and a cropped top accentuated by a fringed suede belt on the hips looks attractive

Brand New Heavies

Not a revival for the 1990s soul band, but
fitness-instructor-speak for January gym joiners
desperate to lose the post-festive flab

Dietribes

Atkins, Scarsdale, Cabbage Soup devotee?
We don't need your rant about how you beat
the bulge… we can eat anything we like and
not put on an ounce

Flabbygasted

The shock and dismay you experience when you try on last summer's clothes and discover that hibernating with a tonne of Cadburys was probably not the smartest way to pass the winter

Flubby

Too much couch-potato behaviour and those extra cals and lack of exercise have left you feeling a trifle Flubby

Fridge Magnets

The sort of irresistible forces that draw you straight to the Smeg when you should really walk on by: chocolate truffles, foie gras, that bottle of Chablis you vowed you'd only pour one glass a day from

Generation XXL

Our supersize-me culture has spawned a whole new breed… Generation XXL

whose idea of exercise is a

Half Marathon

Eating only 50% of a certain rebranded gloopy peanut-filled chocolate bar is your idea of a fitness regime? How we Snicker

Hipposuction

Hun, how did you let it come to this? Forget Gillian McKeith! The only way to lose the Incredible Bulk is emergency Hipposuction

Kosh Nosh

This season's party finger food just has to be Jewish. Kasha Knish, Rugalach, Kneidlach, Bagels and Lox. Just beware of the Matzos... Jerusalem Partichoke! Not fattening at all, goys!

Micro Economics

'Buy one get one free' is your mantra. Fatty,
sugar-laden ready-made meals that can be
chucked in the freezer and heated up in less
than a minute – the mainstay of your sad,
penny-pinching, sofa-bound single life

similarly

Makkro Economics

The same but supersized, from one of those
vast out-of-town food hangars with extra-wide
aisles for extra-wide porkers. Stop watching
Neighbours and waddle down to your
greengrocer for some salad ingredients and do
you and your blimp-sized clan a favour, missus!

Panic Buttons

You thought you'd wear last summer's Helmut Lang skinny suit. Something wrong? It won't do up. Eeek! Panic Buttons! Sorry, tubs, but we can't offer closure on this one

Pauncho

What you get from eating too many tortillas, enchiladas and chimichangas, amigos. That purple poncho you bought in Tijuana should just about cover it

Porkies

Who ate all the pies then? Boutique-speak for dress-size fibbers with delusions of minceur. Sewing a size-10 label into a 16 keeps them sweet

Thinspiration

The pic of a slimmed-down celeb you
pin to your pegboard as encouragement,
Renee Zellweger perhaps, but don't overdo it.
The words Nicole Richie and lollipop-head
come to mind

Toxic Waist

Beat the January bloat. Stick with those diets,
workouts, high colonics and herbal cleansers.
Time to lose that Toxic Waist

Vroom Service

Too tired to cook? A speedy meal on wheels
from your local takeaway is the answer. 'Let's order
Vroom Service!' But night after night? You'll never
see a size 14 again at this rate

Weapons of Mass Reduction

You spend more annually on your arsenal of fat-busting creams and lotions than a small nuclear power does on missiles. Just saying 'no' to that chocolate éclair is a lot cheaper

CELLULITE
BLASTER
100% EFFECTIVE

13

ON EMPLOYMENT

IT'S A 9 TO 5 THING

404

Office-speak for missing, presumed lost.
Based on the internet error message
404 not found. 'Where's the boss's
expenses claim that was on my
desk gone?' '404,' you shrug
sympathetically (having
shredded it earlier
out of sheer malice)

Agenda Bender

The lateral-thinking dork that always lobs in
some out-of-the-box solution just as you were
about to wrap it up and take a long lunch hour

Albatrossing

Unprepared for a meeting, you're winging it big time. Incredibly, the client buys your exceptionally complex proposal and you're landed with it around your neck for the rest of your days

Alpha Geek

He may be the office dork but, when your PC crashes, the Alpha Geek is suddenly your main man

Answer Phoney

You switch to Answer Phoney – 'Sorry, I'm away from my desk, please leave a message' – when you're really reading Heat and basically can't be arsed

Assmosis

Career advancement absorbed by licking the boss's derrière rather than by merit. It sucks but it works

Axecutive Decision

As head of HR, it's your call, mate. It doesn't matter that he's popular, punctual and scrubs up well. He's a lightweight and he's fired!

Bad Curryea Move

Throwing a sickie, blaming last night's dodgy chicken jalfrezi, only to be spotted by the boss's PA as you tuck into a pint and a burger in some beer garden

Bespoke Suit

Headhunter term for a made-to-measure candidate for a senior managerial position. 'I've got the ideal material for that Bespoke Suit you're after.'

Black Collar Worker

Meejah, PRs and creatives. Anyone whose uniform involves polo necks and Armani in a hundred shades of black

Blaggage

It starts off with a few imaginary extra
qualifications on your CV and decades
knocked off your official age. Before long,
you're forever trailing trunkloads of lies in your
wake and won't be due a pension until you're
eighty-seven

similarly

Contouring

Fill in a bit here, snip a little there. Shave off a
few years and generally buff the whole CV up.
But do you seriously imagine recruitment
consultants won't spot the cracks in
the contouring?

Blamestorming

The team managed to miss a deadline, or screw up
a project. Now you all sit around and bitch about
what eejit should carry the can

Bleaching

PR-speak for a damage-limitation exercise. Your dodgy client's sordid extra-marital story leaks out? Spin a sanitised version by big time bleaching it… 'Just a teeny Domestos crisis.'

Blonde Pond

Any office populated by well-groomed identikit dizzy Lizzies with IQs lower than their shoe size. Fashion mags and beauty PR offices are awash with them

Brent Crude

The oily office creep whose line in schoolboy smut and innuendo was surely the template for Ricky Gervais's awesome comic character David

Charbringer of Doom

You're in a great mood until the office
Cassandra delivers a cuppa to your desk,
then proceeds to depress you with an
endless litany of woe

Circling the Drain

On your last chance. One misdemeanour away
from down the plughole, fella

Clockroach

A dead-end-job office insect whose only pleasure is
watching the hands tick round to 5.30

Collateral Dommage

So dropping X in the shit also brings down Y at the same time? Tough! Never liked either of them, really. Caught in the crossfire of office politics? Quel dommage!

Crossrail

What is this miracle future transport solution we keep reading about? Crossrail is already here. Just look at the faces of London commuters sardined on to the 8.14 to Euston

which brings us to

The Crush Hour

Just look at the faces of London commuters sardined on to the 8.14 to Euston. Suddenly Milton Keynes doesn't look so bad.
(OK, maybe not.)

Dashboard Dining

Increasingly frantic schedules rule out long lunches. Juggling a latte and a chicken wrap in the car, we're reduced to dashboard dining, the modern meals on wheels

not to be confused with

Meals on Wheels

No matter how busy your schedule is, munching Maccy D's and the like on public transport is plain gross. It's making us gag, you odious malodorous burgers

Dayhorrea

A quickie after work and you're being bored shitless by a friend intent on sharing the turgid minutiae of their bad day at the office

Director of First Impressions

This job-title one-upmanship is getting out of control. What's so wrong with plain old receptionist then?

Diss-aster Victim

You dish the dirt on the MD to a 'trusted' colleague. Suddenly it's the talk of the office and his secretary's summoned you. You'll be clearing your desk in five, Diss-aster Victim!

The District Line Diet

Step into the hellish travelling sauna at Earl's Court and, by the time it lurches into Aldgate East, you'll have lost four pounds in body fluid

DKTM

No, it's not another Donna Karan diffusion label.
Add it to an email containing bad news – Don't
Kill The Messenger. As in: 'The boss says you
have to work through your lunch hour, for
coming in late again. DKTM.'

Doing Tea

The new power-meeting opportunity. As in: 'The
boss is out with her publicist, Doing Tea.' Faded
grand hotels are the place to do it apparently

Duvet Daze

So you caned it last night and rang in sick?
You're allowed! Snuggle up with tea and
toast to the wonders that are The Jeremy Kyle
Show and Cash In The Attic

E.mauling

Ripping somebody to shreds and forwarding it to every PC in the office… bar theirs, natch

E.Tastrophe

You email dirty-weekend arrangements to your secret lover in marketing, but a slip of the mouse fires it to the office gossip's Inbox instead. Aaagh! E.Tastrophe!

Earbummer

Info or news you don't want to hear. You're flicking through Heat when the boss calls. 'That report needs to be on my desk in five.' Earbummer!

Ego Surfing

Googling yourself up to see what people have been saying about you and then crowing that your name brings up 232,002 results

Ethic Cleansing

You know you were unscrupulous: backstabbing three colleagues, telling a pile of porkies and prickteasing the boss to get that promotion. A means to an end maybe, but a spot of Ethic Cleansing wouldn't go amiss in future. As if!

Heat-Seeking Missile

The office celebrity-by-default can't wait to get her hands on a copy of the weekly C-list sleb bible and drop the bombshell about what Kerry Katona or Colleen McLoughlin did last week. Like we care!

ICE TRAY

Any impersonal sales office where everyone sits in identical anonymous cubicles and spends their day cold calling

Johnny No Stars

A loser. (Based on McDonald's lapel-badge staff-grading system.) 'Eurgh! Go out with that freak from IT? He's a total Johnny No Stars.'

The Magic Roundabout

Commuter speak for the M25 London Orbital – goes around slowly, often gets stuck and, by the time you finally get off it, Zebidee will be saying 'Time for bed!'

MaxC-mise

PR-speak for a potential scandal turned around and milked to maximum effect. Homage to arch media manipulator, Mr Clifford. As in: 'That Premier League goalie caught dogging in a car park with a minor Royal sure got MaxC-mised; they're getting their own TV show out of it.'

Meercat Moment

When every neck in the office simultaneously stretches up and swivels round to clock what is going on

Mental Floss

Crossword puzzles, online chess, word games, sudoku... anything that keeps your mind alert. In our case, that's lusting after the new hottie in marketing and composing poison-pen letters to the boss's hatchet-faced PA

Mousetrapped

Stuck in a dead-end PC-based desk job. As in: 'Working at that call centre sucks. I feel totally Mousetrapped!'

Palm Pilot

Letchy office rake with wandering-hands syndrome. Sadly, he's an occupational hazard. Knee him in the balls and say nuts to you! And, even if he offers a promotion, on no account grin and bare it

Pavement Pow Wow

Huddled in a circle for a quick gossip over a fag outside the office. Outdoor smokes signal that Big Chief Sitting Blair aims to stub us out

Potty Training

Being forced into a two-day course at a dreary conference facility, while some mad Pauline from The League of Gentlemen treats you like inane children, is the type of Potty Training office workers can live without

Salary Sudoku

Trying to juggle the figures so the finances
work out at the end of the month
is a brainteaser
we really loathe

Scapegloat

The smarmy boss's pet has
finally screwed up and there's a
queue to pin the blame on her.
Gleefully watch her squirm,
in her unaccustomed role
as office Scapegloat

Seagull Supervisor

An office line manager, who swoops in, squawks
loudly, craps on everybody and then flies
off again

Spam Frittering

You spend the first half-hour at your desk pretending to deal with important emails, while privately mulling over those get-rich-quick deals (why are they always from Nigeria?) in your Inbox

Surfbored

Slow day at the office, so you hit the web and check out property for sale in Spain, although you can't afford it; Friends Reunited, although you loathed your classmates; and twenty ways with monkfish, although you'll end up ordering pizza. You're just Surfbored

Testiculating

Rather than lose face because you're not sure of your ground, you resort to waving your hands in the air and talking a lot of balls, hoping nobody will rumble you

Uh No Momento

The split-second when you realise you just did something incredibly stupid. Shutting the door with your keys inside, dissing your boss when he's standing behind you, leaving your baby on the bus… that sort of thing

Vertical Snoozing

The art of sleeping upright as you strap hang, semiconscious, into work on the commuter train

Walkie Talkie

Time's too tight for deskbound meetings. Power players do it on the hoof. 'Let's do Walkie Talkie on the way to the car.'

14

ON YOUR MIND

BRAINTEASERS

ad-lib

You are about to swear, then realise your
mother/teacher/boss is present. 'Sugar, Fudge,
Cu… andyfloss!' or similarly sweet Bad-libs
emerge from your dirty gob

Binge Thinking

When your head is one big tumble dryer, filled
with mental dirty laundry on a permanent
negative spin cycle, you're in big trouble. Punch
drunk on Binge Thinking, you need a fortnight's
R & R in the Seychelles, baby!

Brainworm

A sound or thought that burrows its
way into your noodle and
just won't quit

Cashback Flashback

You could swear you got £100 at Tesco's tills
last night. Now you're down to a fiver. You panic
and feverishly rewind your evening to see
where it all went. It's a Cashback Flashback

Emotional Jet Lag

You've been caught up in a crisis, flying high on
adrenaline. Only when the turbulence passes,
do you finally come down to earth with a bump
and feel as drained as if you've done six back-
to-back trips to Los Angeles

Emotional Mezze

Sharing every little traumatic titbit and dishing up
your overspiced love life on a platter for all to share?
Talk about an Emotional Mezze

Fibbertyjibbit

The telltale signs are all there. Hopping from foot to foot, twitching nervously and generally Fibbertyjibbiting… you are such a rubbish liar

Frankophile

She needs to hear: 'Don't worry, there will be an even more fantastic guy along soon, especially with you looking so good lately.' NOT: 'Let's face it, you're not getting any younger and you do need to get down the gym.' Frankophile bluntness. Are you an Aquarian or a Sagittarian by any chance?

Front of Brain

When a previously deep-stored thought pops into your consciousness and becomes a priority. As in: 'I must call my bank manager about upping the overdraft. That's so Front of Brain right now.'

Group Thugging

Peer pressure from mates desperate to convert you to their causes. Resist mob rule: Lost is not the TV show of the century, Pete Doherty is not the new Messiah and it's OK to have a Big Mac

Guilt Trip

He's been off every second weekend on business trips with his PA and now he's suggesting quality time with you at some flashy spa. What's he hiding? And, although you really don't want to go there, you're thinking Guilt Trip

Hard-Boiled Beg

Cynical, ruthless pleading aimed at manipulating one's better nature. Just because you're blonde and gorgeous doesn't mean we can't see through your sob story, lady

In-homme-nia

The inability to sleep when there's man trouble on your mind

consider also

Femmished

The inability to eat when your guts are in knots because your woman has walked out on you (applies mostly to lesbians and hypersensitive males)

and

Perpetual Emotion

Running around like a loony and unable to switch off due to your entire thought process being feverishly dominated by some love-life complication. Not nice

Karmachanics

Ashtanga, meditation, Reiki, Tai chi: whatever it takes to keep you grounded and sane in this mad, mad world

Possibility Paralysis

Big-city stasis. Surrounded by myriad bars, restaurants, clubs and cultural activities, but just can't decide? You end up ordering pizza and watching Heartbeat. This is not why you moved here from the sticks

Psychic Sidekick

The friend you turn to for advice when you need to vibe in on a situation. 'Will John and I stay together?' Er, hello! Like they'd know? Single, jobless and broke, their own life isn't exactly star-crossed bliss.
Gypsy Petulengro, they ain't!

Shampain

Acting all concerned and understanding as they pour their heart out and start to bubble on the phone. Yet, the minute you put the handset down, you're fizzing with excitement about who you can tell first

Skank Account

A blow-by-blow account of a sordid experience. On balance, we prefer not to know what lies deep in your vaults

Spooky Bouquet

All you got from the other half at Christmas was a Kylie CD and some Thornton's choccies. Now, for no apparent reason, he has just presented you with £150 worth of designer blooms. Your mind switches on to suspicion overload, rattled by the Spooky Bouquet

Transcendental Medication

Mumbo jumbo, maybe. But your religious devotion to Amazonian guarana root, Siberian marsh algae and dried Burmese orchid petal is the only thing stopping you from falling apart

15

ON ANON
STUFF THAT DIDN'T FIT
IN ELSEWHERE

Anticipatient

GP-speak for someone who presents with a minor head cold but expects a prescription for antibiotics and a sick note for a fortnight

Barratt House

Dance music by numbers. We don't care if they're remixed by Armand Van Helden, Erick Morillo or Paul Oakenfold… we ain't hitting the floor to any Spice Girl relaunch attempt

Cabinet Reshuffle

Resigned to clearing the shelves of all those past-their-sell-by-date seasonings and exotic herbs you never got round to using, you embark on a Cabinet Reshuffle

Carpetting

It's a pile of metal on four wheels, so please desist from giving your motor a name and talking to it like it's a cutesy furry animal

Cashturbation

Showing off about your six-figure salary, how expensive your designer shoes were, what you spent on your new wheels and the price of your penthouse pad. Wanker!

Claims Farmer

Daytime-TV-advertised, no-win-no-fee service. They sow the seed in your head and harvest big time on ludicrous litigation. Stabbed yourself on a staple at the office? Sue 'em!

Control Freak

Channel-hopping remote fiends that drive you crazy, as they chain flick through their entire cable package. Can we just watch Big Brother in peace please?

Dweddings

'Tis the season for top hats, tails and naff embroidered waistcoats, sneering at pond-life cousins over scampi in a basket and warm Liebfraumilch, doing the Birdie Dance with your auntie Doris and waking up in bed with the Bridesmaid of Dracula the next day. Dwedding it!

Factitious

Just because you say it often enough doesn't make it true. 'I am twenty-nine, 6ft 1in, built like Brad Pitt and got a first at Oxford.' Er, no! Fact is, you're that dumpy middle-aged donut from the post room, matey

Flightmare

With not a seat to spare on the red eye from Florida, you find yourself sandwiched between minging Miami Man Mountains. Flightmare! You knew that hatchet-faced cow at check-in had it in for you

Fortune Cookie

A flaky hostage to fortune that can't face the day without reading their stars, casting the I Ching and reading their own tarot

Happy Crappy

The marvellous relief of parking your harris on a loo, when you've been bursting for ages

Horrorscope

Tailoring some doom-laden drivel you read in a tabloid to fit your pessimistic overview of the day ahead. Sun in Uranus? Pisces off!

G.O.O.D. Gig

Not a Raconteurs or Kaiser Chiefs concert, but
student-speak for any kind of part-time
Get Out Of Debt job which will help pay
off those crippling loans

HERBICIDE

The phenomenon whereby you discover the
supermarket basil, coriander or parsley plant
you bought yesterday has managed
to top itself overnight

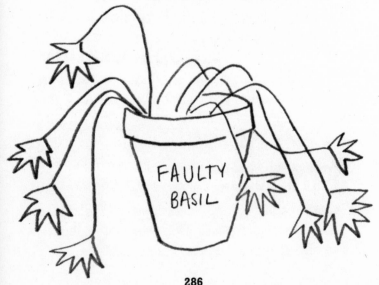

Hyperventilating

You swore you'd given up. Now you're rushing around and opening windows, spraying rooms with expensive pong and flapping your hands at a lingering pall of smoke, in case you're rumbled for having a crafty fag

Kitchen Stink Drama

Having another major set-to about who'll clean up a whole week's worth of minging dishes? Spare us the Kitchen Stink Drama and buy a dishwasher… or hire staff

Monkey Bath

A bath so scalding it makes you yelp: 'Ooh! Hoo! Ooh! Ah! Ah! Ah!' as you gingerly ease yourself in

Multiple Choregasm

When getting off on spring-cleaning becomes a substitute for sex, we worry about you. This is not what we call suitable domestic-goddess behaviour

Mutt Morph

Inevitable tendency for dog owners to turn into their pooches. Does Laurence Llewellyn-Bowen own a spaniel?

Need Jerk Reaction

Their partner snapped at them. Their pet is unwell. They broke a nail. Who cares? Moaning attention-seeking mates' Need Jerk Reactions are bringing us down

Obitchery

Witty, barbed, venomous review that goes in for the kill and leaves its subject for dead. Julie Burchill is still queen of the media assassins

Personal Jesus

Trainer, dietician, spiritual guru, holistic therapist and stylist rolled into one. How did you ever survive without your own Personal Jesus?

Plumbing the Depths of Disrepair

Given that you cost more than a Marc Jacobs coat, is it too much to ask that you actually fix our broken ball cock? Cowboy plumbers drive us round the S bend

PMT

Time of the month? Let's talk about time of the week. Blokes suffer from it too, y'know… especially when their team are up against Man U or Chelsea. Pre-match tension, that is

Post Analysis

Picking up a just delivered letter and examining the unfamiliar handwriting, holding it up to the light and trying to decipher the postmark. Just open the damn thing!

Ring of Ire

The tidemark your filthy inconsiderate flatmate leaves around the bath for you to clean up. 'If you want me to act as a skivvy, cough up some cash, Johnny!'

San Pancracio Fa Mi Spazio!

A very useful Italian appeal to the patron saint of parking spaces. He'll find you a meter and it works every time. If the Vatican's marketing men can come up with a few more, we'll all be keeping the faith. Santa Valeria… is she owt to do with the lotteria?

Schaggenfreude

The satisfaction gained from learning that your fabulously attractive mate's sex life is even less exciting than yours is

to be discussed with

A Schadenfreunde

The mate you automatically call to share 'guess what?' news with: 'Sophie got sacked from her £100k job and came home to find her husband in bed with some bloke from his rugby team. It's too, too ghastly,' you snigger

Slap Dash

Slobbing around at home à la Vicky Pollard,
when the beau, or, worse, your bitchy friend,
rings to say they'll drop by for tea in five. It's the
Slap Dash for you, as you frantically trowel the
war paint on

Soupernanny

You're swinging a couple of sickies. Both the
office and your family swallowed the bad-flu
routine. Then, just when you're getting comfy on
the sun lounger, your ancient granny shows up
with some homemade pea and ham. Aw, bless!

Tom Tom (Go) Club

Turn off those annoying computer-generated-
voice satellite navigation dashboard devices:
'Turn left. Turn right. You have arrived at your
destination.' Getting from Piccadilly Circus
to Hyde Park Corner isn't exactly the
Paris–Dakar rally, is it?

T.Rex Syndrome

Old gits suddenly springing to life when the DJ drops a 70s rock track at a party. Random uncontrolled jerking motions accompanied by shouting at the tops of their voices. You are so 20th century, boy

Trolley Tango

Can Tesco, Asda et al. fix those effing wheels? We want a swift supermarket sweep, not a partner for Strictly Come Dancing

Trolley Troll

Hatchet-faced cabin-crew dragon that'll bang your leg every time she passes with the drinks cart and 'accidentally' pour scalding coffee over you when you hit turbulence

Weecology

A morbid fascination about what the
colour of your urine says about your health.
Hands up everyone who thinks Gillian McKeith
is a load of pish!

Widdle Waddle

The frantic 'holding it all in' stance
adopted by those who are desperate for a
wee, pissed off that there's nowhere
around to relieve themselves.
At last, a reason to visit McDonald's

16

ON THE FIRST DAY
OF CHRISTMAS

A Wayne in a Manger

The Chav school nativity play.
Starring Kyleigh-Jade as Mary
and Mitchell as Jesus

or

A Wean in a Manger
Same us above, but set in Glasgow

Mistle Tony

At the Crimbo party, the office sleazeball corners you under the dreaded berries, then snogs you senseless. Horror of horrors, after only three gins, you're actually enjoying it

Mrs Claws

Beware the office gossip. Armed with
damaging scandal after the staff party,
she'll have a festive field day ripping
your reputation to shreds

PINtomime

What a performance! It's Christmas Eve
and the merry office partygoer forgets his
PIN. The ATM swallows his sole cash card,
meaning your prezzie ain't happening. Quel
drag! That Prince Charming act won't work
when this sister turns ugly

Rank Xerox

It's the morning after the office Christmas bash
and some joker has put a photocopy of Bob
from Bought Ledger's lardy behind on your
desk. Oooh! Rank Xerox!

Santa's Grotto

The Beckham's 'Intimately' fragrance for men, cartoon socks & tie set, Il Divo DVD and Rudolph the Red-nosed Reindeer golf club covers not on your Crimbo wish list? Cash refunding Santa's Grotto is a tiresome but necessary post-Christmas tradition

Santa's Sacked

For bringing you more slippers, a Dyson, a perfume you wouldn't fumigate a flea-ridden dog with and a bleedin' Natasha Bedingfield CD

Twinkle Toastie

Christmas Eve, the wee ones are in bed, the tree lights sparkle and you're snuggling up in front of the fire, all Twinkle Toastie. Say... aaah!

Yule Grinner

With a rictus smile, Yule Grinners dispense goodwill to relatives, colleagues and small children, while secretly dreaming of behaving more like Billy Bob Thornton's awesome Bad Santa

and finally

Hogmoany

'Restaurants are a rip-off. Clubs will be too crazy. The street party will be yobbo central. We'll never get a taxi, etc. But I don't want to stay in on New Year's Eve.' Really? Got a better idea, you Hogmoany horror?

The J-Lo

January 2nd. It's cold. It's dark and Easter's months away. Ah well, Happy New Year anyway!